W9-BRL-511

WITHDRAWN

CHARLESTON COUNTY LIBRARY

NATIONAL
GEOGRAPHIC
KiDS

Absolute Expert

SOCCER

All the
LATEST
FACTS From
the Field

Eric Zweig

With professional referee
Mark Geiger

NATIONAL GEOGRAPHIC
Washington, D.C.

CONTENTS

FOREWORD by soccer expert and professional referee Mark Geiger 6

CHAPTER 1
Playing the Game   8

Expert Introduction 10
Changing the Laws 15
Talk the Talk 16
Time After Time 19
Laying Down the Law 22
Fielding Your Team 26
Yellow and Red Cards 28
Get in the Game 30

CHAPTER 2
The Origins of Soccer   32

Expert Introduction 34
Ancient Roots in China 36
Sports in Ancient Egypt 38
Greeks and Romans 38
The World's Oldest Soccer Ball 40
English Soccer in the Middle Ages ... 42
Mob Football 44
The Game Starts to Take Shape 46
A Different Type of Football 48
Get in the Game 52

CHAPTER 3

Soccer Around the World   54

Expert Introduction............................ 56
Rule Britannia 58
How Soccer Spread 60
World Cup By the Numbers 66
FIFA Rules the World........................ 68
How the World Cup Started 70
How the World Cup Works Today 74
Soccer's Six Zones............................ 76
Get in the Game 78

CHAPTER 4

Soccer in North America   80

Expert Introduction............................ 82
The MLS Story.................................... 84
MLS Teams 88
David Beckham and MLS.................... 93
Early American Soccer Leagues 96
Women's Soccer History.................... 100
Women's Soccer in the
United States..................................... 102
Get in the Game 106

MORE READING AND
QUOTATIONS CREDITS 108
INDEX 109
PHOTO CREDITS 111

MARK GEIGER

FOREWORD

For as long as sport has been an important part of our society, millions of adults and children have dreamed about putting on a uniform to compete. Some soccer clubs around the world have a history that spans more than 100 years, and the loyalty of fans for their clubs rivals that which they feel for their national team. Playing for your club or for your country is a goal that few athletes ever achieve, but with this accomplishment comes a huge responsibility to the team and to the fans as well. Fans can feel the heartache and the pain in a loss just as much as the players do, and when the team wins, everyone—players and fans alike—celebrates in victory.

My name is Mark Geiger, and while I'm not a professional soccer player, I do get to occupy the best seat in the house at every game. I'm a referee. I've been officiating games in Major League Soccer since 2004 and have been fortunate enough to represent the United States on the international stage since 2008. In 2012, I was selected to go to the London Olympic Games, and, in 2014, my own dreams were realized when I was selected to referee at the FIFA World Cup in Brazil.

As a referee, I don't have the same stresses that the players feel during the game. The pressure to win for the fans, to score the winning goal, or to make the big save are things I don't experience. However, we referees have our own set of stresses. Players and coaches can make mistakes. Not every pass reaches its target, and not every shot becomes a goal. The referee is the only one on the field who is not allowed to make a mistake. Whether it's calling a foul that leads to a penalty kick, raising the flag for offside to wipe out a goal, or giving a red card for a challenge, every decision is intense. Then add the fact that the referees in big games must make these decisions in less than one second with over 80,000 spectators screaming, and with millions watching multiple replays and different camera angles on TV. No, it's not the same pressure the players face, but it is extremely stressful. Still, it's an experience that I dreamed for years about being a part of.

For players and referees alike, playing on the big stage is a thrill only a few will ever get. I've been fortunate in my career to have worked in legendary stadiums like Wembley and Old Trafford during my time at the Olympic Games, and the Maracanã during the World Cup. Coming out of the tunnel for the introduction with the FIFA anthem playing is an indescribable feeling. The first time I experienced this—seeing the waves of colors for the two teams, and hearing the deafening cheers of the sold-out crowd—I was overcome by a wave of emotions I can't really put into words. I knew that every decision I made could have a huge impact on the result of the game and possibly even on how the tournament played out. It was difficult, but these are experiences I would never trade. As I said, I had the best seat in some of the best stadiums with the best players in the world ... and it's all been very exciting! So look for me throughout this book as I share my knowledge about soccer—the most popular game in the world.

—Mark Geiger

REFEREE MARK GEIGER IN ACTION

TWO BOYS IN ASIA
PRACTICE SOCCER.

CHAPTER 1
PLAYING THE GAME

INTRODUCTION

MANY YOUNG PLAYERS AROUND THE WORLD

look up to professional athletes. These athletes are idolized, and they become role models. You see their jerseys proudly worn in the halls at school; on the streets, parks, and fields around town; and in the stands at games. Kids grow up trying to be like their heroes, acting and playing the way they do.

MARK GEIGER

So, what does it take to make it to the highest level in sports? What do young players need to do to be the very best they can be? As with anything we do in life, you must practice. If you want to be a better reader, read more books. If you want to be a better piano player, work on technique and keep playing the difficult pieces. If you want to be a better soccer player, work on your skills.

Most of the world's greatest athletes begin their sports at a very young age. They work very hard to become better and better. It takes years of hard work and dedication to be among the very best. In fact, it's said that to become an expert at anything, you must do it for more than 10,000 hours. That's a lot of practice!

There's a very small difference between good soccer players and great ones. The players who are viewed as the very best have outstanding individual skill. They are able to trap the ball well and control it with their first touch. They're able to keep the ball close to them while dribbling, keep their head up, and change their moves in order to deceive their opponents and dribble around them. These are skills you can practice. You don't even need a group of people to work with. All you need is a ball. Are you going to be able to perform tricks like Ronaldo on your very first try? Of course not! But that's why you practice. You try, and try again until you master the skills. The more you develop your individual skills as a player, the better you'll be when you get in a group setting—and the better you'll make your whole team.

Natural talent helps a lot, but you'll probably find that the more you practice, the more talent you have! There's no reason why you cannot make yourself the best player you can possibly be. So, grab a ball, go out to your backyard or a park, and practice. Shoot the ball at a wall, trying to hit a specific target. Control the ball when it rebounds back to you. Dribble the ball, keeping your head up and looking around at your surroundings. Practice the trick moves you see your favorite players performing. If you put in the work, who knows? Maybe someday you will be the player whose jersey is on the back of every young player! As a professional ref, I've seen it all, and I'm very excited to share some of my experiences with you throughout this book!

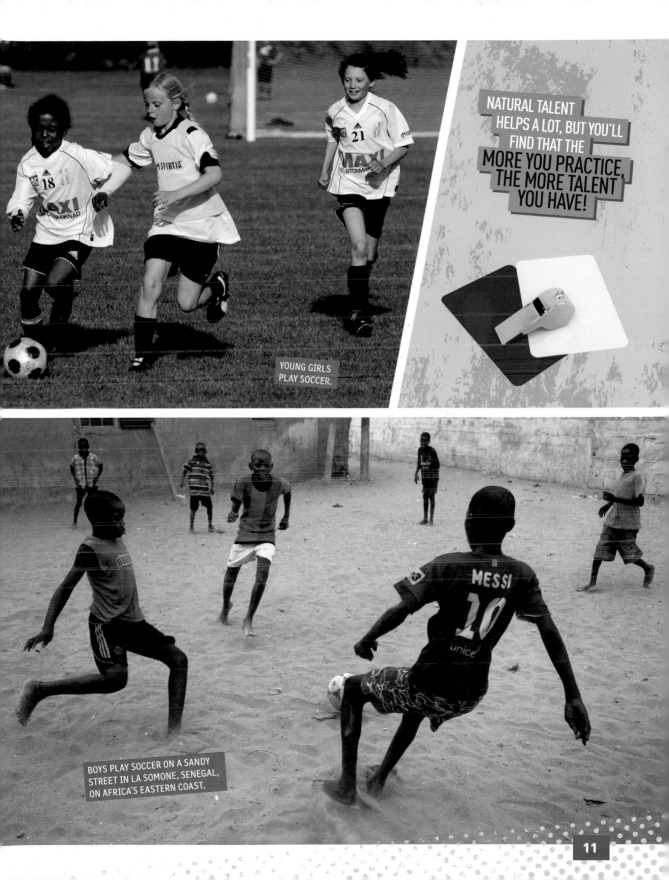

YOUNG GIRLS PLAY SOCCER.

NATURAL TALENT
HELPS A LOT, BUT YOU'LL
FIND THAT THE
MORE YOU PRACTICE,
THE MORE TALENT
YOU HAVE!

BOYS PLAY SOCCER ON A SANDY
STREET IN LA SOMONE, SENEGAL,
ON AFRICA'S EASTERN COAST.

FOR MOST OF ITS HISTORY, SOCCER WAS PLAYED WITHOUT ANY SET RULES—AND SOMETIMES IT JUST BARELY RESEMBLED THE SPORT WE CALL SOCCER TODAY.

So how did soccer go from kicking a ball around to having all the rules that we now know and love today? Short answer: It didn't happen overnight.

In England in the 17th, 18th, and early 19th centuries, each school's teams would play by their own rules. As soccer grew in popularity, this started to become a problem. Especially when graduates from the many different public schools—British private schools—would get together at university. If they wanted to play soccer, what kind of soccer game would they play? Everyone wanted to play by the rules they were used to! "The result was dire confusion," said a former student at Cambridge University when he remembered a game played there in 1839. "Every man played the rules he had been accustomed to at his public school. I remember how the Eton men howled at the Rugby men for handling the ball."

So, in 1848, a committee of Cambridge men got together to create their own set of rules. Unfortunately, there are no copies of those rules that still exist today. However, there is a set of Cambridge Rules from 1856 that was found in a school library. There were 11 rules in all, but the game they describe is still a lot different than what we'd call soccer today. It seems to be a combination of rugby and soccer. Players weren't allowed to pick up the ball from the ground, but they were allowed to catch the ball out of the air after it had been kicked. It was against the rules to run with it, though. A ball

A COACH GIVES INSTRUCTIONS TO HIS TEAM.

CORNER KICKS WERE ADDED TO SOCCER'S RULES IN 1872.

that was caught had to be kicked away. Players were allowed to throw the ball in from the sidelines after it went out of bounds, but once the ball was in play it was against the rules to kick it to any other player who was farther up the field. And when it came to stopping an opposing player, or trying to get the ball from them, it was against the rules to hold, push, or trip them.

The men at Cambridge were pretty pleased with their new rules ... but they didn't catch on right away. Public school students all over England still liked to play their own games. In 1861, an English magazine called *The Field* (which still exists) published a story about the problems this created. "What happens when a game of football is proposed at Christmas among a party of young men assembled from different schools?" the writer asked. He then went on to describe the various arguments that would break out about whose rules to use. "Thus it is found impossible," the writer said, "to get up a game."

The problem wasn't only with soccer that was being played in schools. Groups of men all across England had begun forming their own

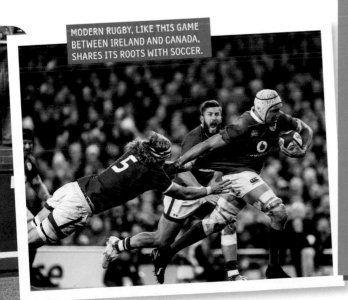

MODERN RUGBY, LIKE THIS GAME BETWEEN IRELAND AND CANADA, SHARES ITS ROOTS WITH SOCCER.

HOW SOCCER GOT ITS NAME

With the creation of the Rugby Football Union in 1871, there were officially two kinds of football in England. To tell them apart more quickly, people began to call Rugby Football "rugger." The game played by the Football Association was officially known as Association Football, but people shortened it to "soccer" from the letters *s-o-c* in Association. In England, Rugby Football would come to be known simply as rugby, so Association Football was just called football. But in North America, rugby was already starting to change into the game we call football, so soccer stayed as soccer.

soccer clubs for games and for exercise. They didn't know which rules to use, either. Ebenezer Cobb Morley had never attended a public school, but he was smart. Morley was a lawyer in London and lived in the London suburb of Barnes. He was also a soccer player and captain of the Barnes Club. Morley was a man who liked to get things done, and so he organized a meeting in London on October 26, 1863.

Eleven London soccer clubs sent representatives to Morley's meeting. Many public schools were invited to attend, but only one sent someone to the meeting. The group decided to call itself the Football Association. It took a few more meetings to get things

sorted out, but on December 8, 1863, the Football Association approved a new set of rules that had been written by Ebenezer Morley. They were known as the Laws of the Game.

The Football Association, or the FA as it's usually called, is still in charge of soccer in England. But it didn't get off to a very good start. Like the Cambridge Rules a few years before, Morley's new Laws of the Game actually tried to come up with a sport that was a combination of rugby and soccer. It didn't work out very well. Rugby teams weren't very happy, and the soccer clubs in the northern part of England still preferred their own laws, which were known as the Sheffield Rules. Even many of the teams in London ignored the new laws

RULES OF THE **Association Football Players' and Trainers' Union.**

THE ORIGINAL FA BOOK CONTAINING THE LAWS OF THE GAME

PLAY BY THE RULES

MARK GEIGER

ALTHOUGH EVERY COUNTRY AND EVERY NATIONAL TEAM today plays by the same set of rules, the style of the game can be very different. You only need to turn on the TV and watch games from around the world to see that the way the game is played can look very different from region to region and team to team. Some of the teams are very calculating and tactical in their approach to a game. Other teams are very direct. You will see teams that are very aggressive and physical, while others move the ball quickly, avoiding contact and challenges with opponents. There are teams that like to attack, and others that hang back to concentrate on defense.

One of FIFA's most important jobs is to help train referees from every country in order to make sure that,

even when the styles are different, the Laws of the Game are applied and enforced the same way. This way, whenever teams from different parts of the world play each other, they all know the Laws they will be playing by and how they will be called by the referee.

A REFEREE TRAINS PRIOR TO A YOUTH TOURNAMENT IN CHINA.

of the Football Association and continued to play their own games.

It took until the early part of the 1870s for the Football Association to truly make its mark. Probably the biggest part of that was the creation of the FA Cup, a national championship tournament that began during the 1871–72 season and continues in England to this day. But even the FA Cup may not have made a difference if it wasn't for another key move by the Football Association a few years earlier, in 1866. That was the year the FA realized it was impossible to please everyone and decided to make some key changes to its rules. Players would now be allowed to pass the ball to players in front of them. A crossbar was added to the top of the goal, and points would be scored only if the ball went between the posts and under the bar. (Early crossbars seem to have been made of tape! More permanent crossbars don't appear to have existed until about 1875.) Catching the ball would now be illegal. After 1870, players wouldn't even be allowed to knock the ball down with their hands anymore. They'd have to use their heads, as players in Sheffield had been doing for years.

Not surprisingly, rugby players weren't very happy with the rule changes. In 1871, a meeting was held with 21 rugby clubs that got together to form the Rugby Football Union. With that, soccer had finally become its very own sport.

Changing the Laws

But times change, and so do the ways we play sports. Since the FA changed Ebenezer Cobb Morley's original Laws of the Game in the 19th century, there have been many more additions and changes made to the official rules of the game. So, who gets to create the new laws, or make changes to the ones that already exist?

FANS HAVING FUN IN JOHANNESBURG, SOUTH AFRICA

SUPPORT YOUR TEAM

ALL SPORTS FANS ARE A LITTLE BIT CRAZY. After all, "fan" is just a short form of the word "fanatic," which means "a person with an intense interest and enthusiasm." Still, soccer fans often seem to be more intensely interested than other sports fans! In some cities, fans will parade through the streets to the stadium, and fans all around the world are known for dressing up in their team colors. Team scarves are especially popular all over the world. Soccer fans also love to sing! Like so much about the game, this tradition began in Britain, where entire stadiums packed with fans will sing together throughout the game. Sometimes, they sing the words to real songs, and sometimes they sing songs with words written especially for their teams. Many fans will bang on drums during games, but the noise they make is nothing like the noise from a plastic horn known as a vuvuzela. During the 2010 World Cup in South Africa, the buzzing noise from stadiums full of fans blowing their vuvuzelas was so loud it was even hard to watch the games on television! Vuvuzelas are so noisy that many stadiums around the world have banned fans from using them.

MARK GEIGER

TALK THE TALK

Every sport has its own words that are unique to the game. Soccer is no exception. Brush up on some of these terms!

ATTACKER: The player who has the ball.

BICYCLE KICK: A move in which a player kicks the ball backward over his or her own head. Often both feet are off the ground in a sort of jumping somersault.

BOOKED/BOOKING: The noting by the referee of a player's name or number for receiving a yellow card.

BOX: The box is another name for the penalty area.

BREAKAWAY: A move in which an attacker has possession of the ball and gets behind all the defensive players to move in alone on the goalkeeper.

CAP: Every time a player plays a game for his or her national team it's referred to as earning a cap. Men on England's national team still receive an actual hat for games they play.

CAUTION: When players receive a yellow card, it is said that they have been "cautioned."

CLEAR: To kick or head the ball away from the goalmouth and end another team's scoring chance.

CROSS: A long pass often in the air that is made toward the middle of the field.

DRAW: When a game ends in a tie score.

DIVE: An exaggeration of the effect of being contacted by an opponent to try and influence the referee to award a free kick. An intentional dive can earn a player a yellow card.

DRIBBLE/DRIBBLING: The skill of controlling the ball with your feet as you move about the field.

EXTRA TIME: A method of trying to decide a winner when regulation time has ended in a draw. In most other sports, this is called overtime.

FEINT/FEINTING: A move that is made to trick or confuse an opponent so that you can get around them.

HEAD/HEADING/HEADER: An attempt to pass, clear, control, or shoot the ball with your head (usually your forehead).

HEEL: To pass the ball directly backward, often with the heel of your foot.

KIT: The standard equipment and uniform worn by a player.

MARK: To cover a player who may or may not have the ball; to prevent a player from receiving the ball. A defender who is guarding an opponent is said to be "marking" that player.

MATCH: A British term used instead of the word "game." Soccer matches are sometimes referred to as fixtures, as well.

NIL: Zero or nothing. It's a common British term that is often used in saying soccer scores.

OWN GOAL: When a player scores a goal into his or her own net.

PITCH: This is an English word to describe a sports field. It's quite common in soccer to call the field a pitch.

PACE: The speed of a player or the ball.

TACKLE: To use your feet in an attempt to take the ball away from an opposing player. A tackle may sometimes involve bumping a player with a shoulder, but there must be no holding, pushing, tripping, elbowing, or hip-checking.

SUPPORTERS: People who like soccer or a soccer team are often called supporters instead of fans.

TOUCH: Contact with the ball with any part of the body (except the arms and hands) is called a touch. Touch can also refer to how well you control the ball.

TOUCHLINES: Touchlines in soccer are like the sidelines in American football. A ball that goes out of play over the sidelines is said to have gone into touch.

TRAVEL TEAM: An American term for a serious youth or junior soccer program where the team regularly travels out of state or town to play games.

The Football Association still plays a big part in the decisions. In fact, all of the early British associations still have a lot to say.

Since 1886, representatives from the soccer federations of England, Northern Ireland, Scotland, and Wales have formed the International Football Association Board (known as the IFAB) to oversee the rules of the game. Fédération Internationale de Football Association (FIFA), the group that governs soccer around the world, became a member of the IFAB in 1913, but the groups from Britain still had the most to say about any rule changes. All the way up until 1958, the UK groups could vote together to change the Laws of the Game even if FIFA didn't agree. Nowadays, England, Ireland, Scotland, and Northern Ireland each get one vote on the IFAB, while FIFA gets four votes. It takes six out of eight votes to make a change to the Laws of the Game, so even if all of the UK groups want to change something, they have to convince two of the FIFA voters. And, if all four FIFA voters want to make a change, they still have to convince two of the UK voters. It makes things a lot more fair.

The IFAB gets together every year to review the Laws of the Game and to discuss any changes. Even though FIFA and the four UK countries are the only ones who get to vote, all of the national federations around the world, or any of the international regional zones, are allowed to make suggestions. All proposals to make changes are discussed and voted on. If any changes are made to the Laws, they will become part of the way soccer is played all around the world.

FIFA LOGO

CELEBRATING A GOAL

TOSSING A COIN TO CHOOSE SIDES

Law 11, about Offside—when a player is in the opponent's end of the field—has probably changed more than any other rule in the sport's long history. When the first 13 Laws were written by the Football Association in 1863, Offside was rule #6. At the time, every player in front of the ball was considered offside! That meant there was no forward passing at all. Without forward passing, it was hard to score goals, so the Law was changed for the first time in 1866. The new rule said that any player in front of the ball would not be offside as long as there were three players from the other team between them and the opponent's goal.

Other changes were coming. In 1881, it was decided that no one would be offside on a corner kick. In 1907, it was decided that no player would be considered offside when they were on their own half of the field. Since 1920, there have been no offsides on throw-ins. The biggest change came in 1925 when the Law about offside was changed to say that only two players, instead of three, had to be between a player and the goal line on a forward pass. That has remained the Law ever since, although another important adjustment was made in 1990. Since then, a player only has to be even with the second-to-last defending player to be considered onside.

Here are a few key changes to other Laws of the Game over the years:

- 1869 – lines were added to the field to mark out the goal area
- 1871 – one player on each team had to be a goalkeeper
- 1872 – corner kicks were introduced
- 1891 – penalty kicks were added
- 1912 – goalies cannot use their hands outside of the penalty area
- 1958 – the use of substitute players is allowed
- 1970 – introduction of red and yellow cards

Time After Time

Soccer is very different from many other sports in that from the opening whistle to the end of

AN ACROBATIC THROW-IN

ADDING SIX MINUTES OF EXTRA TIME

FOULED BY THE GOALKEEPER

THE REFEREE SHOWS A RED CARD.

each half, the clock never stops running. In other sports, such as football, basketball, or hockey, the clock can—and does—stop often. That's not the case in soccer.

Years ago, when the clock hit 45 minutes, the half was over. This became a problem for teams and referees because when the score was close, many teams would find creative ways to waste time. They might fake injuries, or celebrate too long after a goal. Anything in order to wind down the clock and stop the other team from having a chance to score. One resource the referees had to speed up play was to give a yellow card to players who were clearly wasting time. But the best way to help referees fix this situation was to give them the authority to add time to the end of each half to make up for any delays.

According to the Laws of the Game, there are specific reasons that a referee can add time to the end of a half:

- Substitutions
- Assessment and/or removal of injured players
- Wasting time
- Disciplinary sanctions
- Stoppages for drinks or other medical reasons permitted by competition rules

However, the referee also has the authority to add time for other reasons, too. There have been situations in MLS games where flares and other objects were thrown onto the field, laser pointers were being shined in players' faces from the stands, and spectators ran onto the field during play in order to hug or get an autograph from their favorite player. In all these cases, the referee had to add the time lost to the end of the half. But how does the referee know how much time to add? To many people watching, it's a complete mystery why the referee

CHELSEA CELEBRATES A BIG GOAL AGAINST MANCHESTER UNITED.

decides to play a given amount of time. There is nothing in the Laws of the Game that stipulates exactly how much time is to be added; it simply says "allowance is made by the referee in each half for all time lost in that half." So how does the referee know?

Most of the time lost in a half is due to substitutions and injuries. As a rule of thumb, a substitution lasts 30 seconds on average, and an injury lasts approximately one minute. But they are not all the same. Off the field, between the two teams' benches, there is a fourth official. In addition to their prescribed duties, many referees ask the fourth official to help determine how much stoppage time to add. It's easy for the fourth official to look at the clock and determine exactly how long a substitution took or how long it took to evaluate and remove an injured player. The fourth official can also determine how long a cooling break took on those very hot days when one is needed. These times are conveyed to the referee, and with this information, he or she determines how much time to add.

Once the referee determines how much time will be added to the half, the fourth official displays this number to the teams and the spectators using the substitution board. It's important to note that this is not the exact number of minutes that will be added, but the minimum number of minutes left to be played. If there are additional stoppages in the added time, like another substitution, the referee can add a little more time.

The most important thing for the players and the spectators is to have as much action as possible during a game. We want to see the ball in play so the players can play and the fans can cheer on their team. While there are natural stoppages in a game, prolonged stoppages can disrupt the flow of the game and chip away at the time the ball is actually in play. Stoppage time is a way for a referee to help ensure that time is not lost due to long periods when play is stopped and that the complete time of each half is played in the end.

Laying Down the Law

Although it takes a lot of skill to play it well, soccer is one of the simplest games in the world. All you really need to play it is a ball and a space large enough to kick it around. It doesn't have to be a stadium or an official soccer field. You don't even need a lot of rules if you're just playing around with your friends. However, if you're going to play on a team in a league— whether it's just a local club for fun, or a national team going after the World Cup—you're going to need to know the official rules, called the Laws of the Game.

There were originally 13 Laws of the Game written by Ebenezer Cobb Morley when England's Football Association was established in 1863. By 1898, the rules had grown to include 17 Laws.

Today, almost 120 years after Morley's first rules, there are still just 17 Laws of the Game. However, today they involve a lot more details and explanation than they used to.

Law 1: The Field of Play
• The field can be natural grass, artificial turf, or a "hybrid" combination of the two.
• The color of an artificial surface must be green.
• The field must be rectangular in shape and be marked with lines to guide the play.

Law 2: The Ball
• The ball must be round and made of an approved material.
• It must be between 27 and 28 inches (68–70 cm) in circumference and weigh between 14 and 16 ounces (410–450 g).

ONLY THE GOALKEEPER CAN CATCH THE BALL.

A PROFESSIONAL SOCCER BALL MUST BE BETWEEN 27 AND 28 INCHES IN CIRCUMFERENCE AND WEIGH BETWEEN 14 AND 16 OUNCES.

Law 3: The Players

- Each team can have 11 players on the field; one must be a goalkeeper.
- A game cannot start or continue if either team has fewer than seven players.
- This law also covers the substitution of players.

Law 4: The Players' Equipment

- Players must wear a shirt with sleeves, short pants, socks, shin guards, and footwear.
- Goalkeepers are allowed to wear long pants.
- Players cannot wear anything dangerous, or any items of jewelry.

Law 5: The Referee

- One referee controls the game with other officials and enforces the Laws.
- The referee acts as the timekeeper and punishes players who break the rules.

Law 6: The Other Match Officials

- Other match officials (two assistant referees, a fourth official, two additional assistant referees, and a reserve assistant referee) can be used to help the referee control the game.

Law 7: The Duration of the Match

- A game lasts for 90 minutes, split into two equal halves of 45 minutes.
- The referee can add extra time at the end of each half for reasons such as injuries, goal celebrations, or other delays.

MARK GEIGER

BREAKING THE LAW

LAW 1 STATES THAT FOR OFFICIAL LEAGUE GAMES, the field must measure between 100 yards and 130 yards (90–120 m) in length along the touchline and between 50 and 100 yards (45–90 m) in width along the goal line. For international matches, the length must be between 100 yards and 120 yards (100–110 m) long and 70 to 80 yards (64–75 m) in width. Official goals are 8 feet high (2.44 m) and 8 yards wide (7.32 m). But there are several ways that the Laws of the Game are allowed to change depending on who's playing. For games involving youth players under the age of 16, women, or veteran players over age 35, changes are allowed to any or all of these things:

- size of the playing field
- size, weight, and material of the ball
- width and height of the goalposts and crossbar
- length of the game
- number of substitutions

Law 8: The Start and Restart of Play

- A kick-off starts both halves of a match, both halves of extra time, and restarts play after a goal has been scored.
- A coin toss decides who will defend which end and which team will kick off to start the game.
- All players, except the kicker, must be on their own half of the field for every kick-off.

Law 9: Ball In and Out of Play
- The ball is in play at all times except when it has passed completely across the goal line at either end or the touchline on either side.
- The ball is also out of play when the game has been stopped by the referee for any reason.

Law 10: Determining the Outcome of a Match
- A goal is scored when the entire ball has crossed the goal line between the posts and beneath the crossbar.
- The team that scores the most goals wins.
- If both teams score no goals or the same number of goals, the game is a draw (tie).

Law 11: Offside
- A player is offside when he or she is in the opponent's end of the field and any part of his or her body is closer to the opponent's goal than the ball or the second-to-last defending player. (This is usually the last defensive player in front of the goalkeeper.)

  This rule prevents players from hanging around the other team's net and trying to score easy goals.

Law 12: Fouls and Misconduct
- Fouls and misconducts are penalized with cautions, sending players off the field, or awarding the other team direct free kicks, penalty kicks, or indirect free kicks. Offenses include kicking an opponent, tripping, tackling, holding, spitting, touching the ball, and entering the field without permission.

AN OBVIOUS FOUL

BOOKING IT

In today's soccer games, you will sometimes see a referee displaying a yellow card or a red card in the air. A yellow card is a warning to a player that he or she has done something wrong. A red card means the player is ejected from the game. (See pages 28–29 for why a player might earn a yellow or red card.) However, these cards were not always a part of the game. In the early days of soccer, if a player did something to earn a warning from the referee, the player was called over to the referee, and the player's name and number were recorded in the referee's notebook. This is why we can still hear commentators and fans saying that a player has been "booked" by the referee.

In the 1966 World Cup, during a game between England and Argentina, a player had been booked and was later ejected from the game. However, the player was not aware that he'd been previously warned. In World Cup and other international matches, the referee doesn't always speak the language of the players. Obviously, this can lead to confusion. After the tournament, Ken Aston—the head of referees for the 1966 World Cup—was at a stoplight in his car when he came up with the idea of using yellow and red cards as universal "caution" and "stop" signs in the game. The cards were used for the first time in the 1970 World Cup. They've been a part of the game ever since.

Law 13: Free Kicks

- There are two types of free kicks: direct and indirect.
- The laws outline when they are awarded (for fouls) and who can take them (which players).

Law 14: The Penalty Kick

- A penalty kick is awarded if a player commits a direct free kick offense inside his or her penalty area.
- A goal may be scored directly from a penalty kick.

Law 15: The Throw-In

- A throw-in is awarded to the opponents of the player who last touched the ball before it crosses over the touchline.
- The thrower must face the field and throw the ball with both hands from behind and over his or her head.
- A goal cannot be scored by a throw-in. An offside cannot be called on a throw-in.

Law 16: The Goal Kick

- A goal kick is awarded when the attacking team kicks the ball across their opponent's goal line but doesn't score a goal.
- The ball is kicked from any point within the goal area by a player of the defending team.

Law 17: The Corner Kick

- A corner kick is awarded when a defending player knocks the ball across his or her own goal line.
- A player on the attacking team kicks the ball back into play. These are dangerous for the defending team, as the player taking the corner kick tries to curve the ball in front of the goal for a good scoring chance.

PENALTY KICK

THE THROW-IN

CORNER KICK

FIELDING YOUR TEAM

➤ GOALKEEPERS
The goalkeeper's main job is to keep the other team from scoring goals. Outside of throw-ins, the goalkeeper is the only player who is allowed to use his or her hands. That's why goalkeepers have to wear different colors from their teammates. Many of them wear gloves, too. This allows them to get a better grip on the ball, and it can help prevent injuries. Goalkeepers need to be great athletes to dive and jump at fast-moving soccer balls. They have to be pretty brave, too!

➤ DEFENDERS
The main job of the defenders is to help their goalkeeper stop the other team from scoring. They usually remain on their own half of the field. Defenders have to be good at taking the ball away from opposing players (which is known as tackling), blocking shots, and intercepting passes.

➤ MIDFIELDERS
As the name suggests, midfielders play in between the defenders and the forwards. Midfielders need to know when they have to fall back to help out on defense or rush forward to help in the attack. They also need to have great endurance because they tend to do a lot more running than any other players.

➤ FORWARDS
Forwards are the players who are positioned closest to their opponent's goal. They are often their team's fastest runners. They need to have quick feet, too! The main job of the forwards is to score goals and create scoring chances for their teammates. The center forward is often called a striker and is usually a team's main goal scorer.

4 DEFENDERS
4 MIDFIELDERS
2 FORWARDS

Once the most common, the 4-4-2 is a defensive-minded formation, with four midfielders working to stop an opposing team's forwards from mounting an attack.

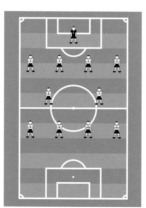

4 DEFENDERS
2 MIDFIELDERS
4 FORWARDS

When a team is behind in the score late in the game, this formation is a strong offensive one, with a team's best goal scorers leading the attack.

3 DEFENDERS
4 MIDFIELDERS
3 FORWARDS

Putting an equal importance on defense and offense, this balanced formation needs a great group of midfielders who can creep back to defend or rush forward to attack.

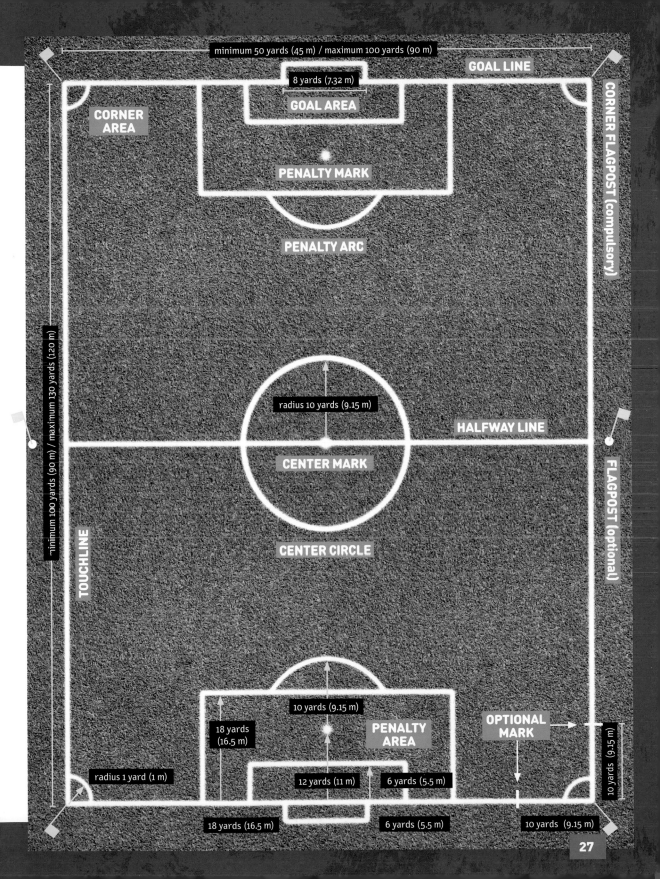

minimum 50 yards (45 m) / maximum 100 yards (90 m)

GOAL LINE

CORNER FLAGPOST (compulsory)

8 yards (7.32 m)

GOAL AREA

CORNER
AREA

PENALTY MARK

PENALTY ARC

minimum 100 yards (90 m) / maximum 130 yards (120 m)

radius 10 yards (9.15 m)

HALFWAY LINE

FLAGPOST (optional)

CENTER MARK

CENTER CIRCLE

TOUCHLINE

10 yards (9.15 m)

18 yards
(16.5 m)

PENALTY
AREA

OPTIONAL
MARK

10 yards (9.15 m)

radius 1 yard (1 m)

12 yards (11 m)

6 yards (5.5 m)

18 yards (16.5 m)

6 yards (5.5 m)

10 yards (9.15 m)

27

YELLOW and RED CARDS

SOCCER IS "THE BEAUTIFUL GAME." However, sometimes, because of the way the players are playing, it's not as beautiful as it should be. When that happens, it's the job of the referee to ensure that soccer is played within the Laws of the Game and to provide a safe environment for the players to showcase their skills.

When players start to play in a manner that is disrespectful to the game, or in a way that is dangerous to their opponents, the referee must try to put a stop to it. Maybe the referee will call a foul or maybe have a word with the player. However, if this doesn't work, or if the situation is bad enough, the referee can display a yellow card (warning) or a red card (ejection) to a player.

MARK GEIGER

THE YELLOW CARD is given to a player to try to get him or her to play within the Laws of the Game again. The Laws list six categories of yellow cards, and within each category, there are specific game situations listed. Here are the categories along with a few of the game situations:

➤➤ **Unsporting Behavior:** This covers a wide variety of offenses. For example, playing in a reckless manner; using your hands to attempt to score a goal; attempting to trick the referee by pretending to have been fouled or hurt; showing a lack of respect for the game.

➤➤ **Dissent:** This is when a player argues over a decision by the referee either in words or through actions.

➤➤ **Persistent Infringement of the Laws of the Game:** This occurs when a player commits several fouls during the game. The shorter the time between fouls, the more likely it is that the player will earn a yellow card.

THE PLAYERS PROTEST A RED CARD.

➤➤ **Delaying the Restart of Play:** Wasting time disrupts the natural flow of the game. Some examples of wasting time that are likely to earn a yellow card are: appearing to take a throw-in but suddenly leaving it to a teammate to take; kicking or carrying the ball away after the referee has stopped play; taking a free kick from the wrong position to force a retake.

➤➤ **Failing to Respect the Required Distance:** During corner kicks, free kicks, and throw-ins, the opposing team must be a certain distance away from the ball. Players run the risk of earning a yellow card if they are too close to their opponent and interfere with the play.

➤➤ **Entering, Re-entering, or Deliberately Leaving the Field of Play Without the Referee's Permission:** There are times that a player must leave the field to correct equipment or receive treatment for an injury. When they do, they must have the referee's permission to come back onto the field. If they run back on without the referee's permission, they will earn a yellow card.

A REAL MADRID PLAYER IS SENT OFF THE PITCH.

THE RED CARD is the most severe type of punishment a player can receive during the course of a game. If a player earns a red card, he or she can no longer participate in the match. The player must leave the field area and must watch the rest of the game from the stands or the locker room. In addition, that player's team must finish the game with one less player on the field, giving their opponents a numerical advantage. Finally, the player earning the red card will be suspended from the team's next match too. This is a big punishment, but you will see that the offenses that earn a player a red card can be equally severe. There are seven categories of red cards in the Laws of the Game, and below is a list of those offenses.

➼ **Serious Foul Play:** A player earns a red card if he or she challenges for the ball using excessive force or in a manner that is dangerous to the safety of the opponent.

➼ **Violent Conduct:** This includes any rough physical act against an opponent, coach, referee, or spectator when not challenging for the ball.

➼ **Spitting at an Opponent or Any Other Person**

➼ **Denying the Opposing Team a Goal or an Obvious Goal-Scoring Opportunity by Deliberately Handing the Ball:** As you know, the only player on the field who can use his or her hands is the goalkeeper. So, when any other player stops the ball from going into the goal by using their hands, it's a serious offense.

➼ **Denying an Obvious Goal-Scoring Opportunity to an Opponent by an Offense Usually Punishable by a Free Kick:** This is normally referred to as DOGSO, and occurs when there is a foul during a one-against-one situation and a goal is the likely outcome.

TRYING TO SCORE ON A FREE KICK

➼ **Using Offensive, Insulting, or Abusive Language and/or Gestures**

➼ **Receiving a Second Caution in the Same Match:** Sometimes, when a player earns a yellow card during a game, he or she does not change the offensive behavior. If this happens, and the player earns a second yellow card (even if it's for a different reason), that player earns a red card and must leave the match.

GET IN THE GAME

EACH YEAR, THE 150,000 REFEREES IN THE UNITED STATES must take a test on the Laws of the Game. Some of the questions are very easy, and some are very difficult. The higher the level of referee you are, the more difficult the test is. How well do you think you will do? Below is a sample of questions from U.S. Soccer's 2016–2017 Entry Level Referee Test, State Referee Test, and National Referee Test. Let's see if you know enough to be the next World Cup referee.

ENTRY LEVEL QUESTIONS

1. A game may not start or continue if either team has fewer than _____ players.
   a. 3
   b. 6
   c. 7
   d. 11

2. An attacking player, in an offside position, receives the ball directly from a teammate's throw-in. Is the player guilty of an offside offense?
   a. Yes
   b. No

3. From a throw-in, the ball goes directly into the opponent's goal without being touched by another player. What is the correct restart?
   a. Corner kick
   b. Goal kick
   c. Throw-in
   d. Kick-off

4. What should the referee do if, during the taking of kicks from the penalty mark, a kicker feints during his or her run prior to reaching the ball and a goal is scored?
   a. Allow the goal
   b. Disallow the goal and retake the kick
   c. Disallow the goal, caution the kicker, and retake the kick
   d. Allow the goal but caution the kicker for unsporting behavior

5. What action should the fourth official take if the referee has issued a second caution to the same player without sending him or her off?
   a. Get the referee's attention immediately to notify him or her of the mistake
   b. Get the assistant referee's attention at the next stoppage and provide the information at that time
   c. Allow the match to continue with the appropriate restart, advising the referee of the mistake at halftime or the end of the game
   d. Ignore the mistake as this issue falls on the referee's shoulders

6. The ball hits the referee in the face and then enters the goal while he or she is temporarily incapacitated. Can the goal be allowed even though the referee did not see it?
   a. No, the referee must have seen the ball completely cross the goal line
   b. Yes, but only if, in the opinion of the other match officials, the goal was scored legally
   c. Yes, but only if, in the opinion of the closest assistant referee, the goal was scored legally
   d. All answers are correct

7. A team deliberately tries to lose a match. What decision should the referee make?
   a. The referee should warn the captain that is this attitude continues, he/she will suspend the match
   b. The referee abandons the match
   c. The referee allows play to continue but includes this fact in his/her post-match report
   d. The referee does not take into account the goals scored during the time this attitude persisted

ANSWERS: Entry Level: 1. c, 2. b, 3. b; State Level: 4. a, 5. a; National Level: 6. b, 7. c

CHAPTER 2

THE ORIGINS OF SOCCER

SCHOOL BOYS PLAY SOCCER IN THIMPHU, BHUTAN.

INTRODUCTION

FOOTBALL, FUTBOL, FUTEBOL, SOCCER.

No matter how you say it or spell it, it's known as "The Beautiful Game." Soccer is played around the world in virtually every country on Earth. There are 211 member associations within FIFA (Fédération Internationale de Football Association), the governing body of soccer.

MARK GEIGER

According to FIFA's latest study, there are approximately 270 million players, coaches, and referees who participate in this wonderful sport. With almost four billion fans worldwide, soccer is by far the most popular sport in the world. As you will see in this chapter, it's one of the oldest, too.

My own personal soccer story began when I was six years old. My mother signed me up to play at the Beachwood Soccer Club near my home in New Jersey, U.S.A. I immediately fell in love with the sport! If I wasn't on the practice field, I was in my yard dribbling the ball and using the space between two large trees, or the markings on my garage, as a goal. Most days, I was either working on my skills with the ball or playing a game with friends. I continued to play and enjoy organized soccer through high school, but unfortunately, I knew I was getting too many nagging injuries to keep on playing at a competitive level. But even when I had to stop playing on teams, my passion and love for the game never died. I remained an active participant through my adult years by playing indoor soccer and by coaching various teams at Lacey Township High School and at the Beachwood Soccer Club.

I really enjoyed playing and coaching, but I knew I would never make it to the professional ranks that way. My greatest contribution to the sport would come as a referee. Even as young as 13 years old, I thought there was no greater job for a teenager than to be out there on the soccer field, taking part in the sport I love as a referee. I started out as all young referees do, officiating games at the under-6 to under-10 level. Since then, I've been fortunate in my referee career to move up the ranks the same way a soccer player does: state cups, regional championships, national championships, semi-professional, professional, and finally, international matches.

Refereeing has become my full-time career. It's brought me to many parts of the world that I may have never seen or experienced otherwise.

Soccer was introduced at different times and in different ways to each part of the globe, but the passion is common all around the world.

CHILDREN PLAY IN EAST TIMOR, A SMALL NATION NEAR AUSTRALIA.

WITH ALMOST 4 BILLION FANS WORLDWIDE, SOCCER IS BY FAR THE MOST POPULAR SPORT IN THE WORLD.

MARK GEIGER

REFEREE MARK GEIGER EXPLAINS THE SITUATION.

ENGLAND BECAME THE BIRTHPLACE OF MODERN SOCCER IN THE MID-1800s, BUT THE SPORT GOT STARTED LONG BEFORE THAT.

Ancient Roots in China

No one really knows if the earliest humans played a game like soccer. Yet there's evidence proving that a game in which players kicked a ball was played in ancient China at least 2,400 years ago. It may be even older than that. Some sources say that games played with balls were popular in China 10,000 years ago!

Ju is an ancient kind of Chinese leather ball that is made of animal skins on the outside and stuffed tightly with hair or bird feathers inside. *Cuju* was a game played using a ju. Cuju means "kick the ball with foot." According to Chinese legends, Cuju was invented by the Yellow Emperor, one of the early heroes of ancient China. Also known as Huangdi, the Yellow Emperor is thought to have been born around 2704 B.C.—nearly 5,000 years ago. In traditional Chinese accounts, he is seen as a wise man who improved the lives of his people. Though he wished to be a peaceful ruler, the Yellow Emperor lived in a time of warfare. It's said he invented the bow and arrow, as well as other early weapons, and his army was able to keep other warring armies in line. It's also said that he invented Cuju to help train his soldiers. As in modern soccer, hands and arms were not allowed to be used to advance the ball, and goals were scored by kicking the ball through two posts.

CUJU IN ANCIENT CHINA

CUJU MEANS "KICK THE BALL WITH FOOT."

MODERN PLAYERS RE-CREATE CUJU.

Cuju remained a popular game in China for several centuries. It became popular during the Han dynasty (206 B.C. to A.D. 220). The Han dynasty is considered a peaceful time in China. Without wars to fight, the Chinese army spent a lot of time playing Cuju. Special playing fields were set aside. There was even a referee. A Han emperor, Wudi, enjoyed Cuju so much that he often asked people to print articles about the games for him. Could these have been the world's first sportswriters? If they were, they probably weren't writing the same kinds of sports stories we read today. Ancient texts on Chinese games didn't really provide play-by-play accounts. They were more like philosophy lessons. Chinese writers liked to compare Cuju's round ball and square field to Yin and

CUJU BALL MADE FROM HAIR

Yang, ancient concepts of harmony and balance. But some of these stories do help explain the way they game was played. They describe one big difference between the ancient games of this time period and today's soccer: Goals were scored by shooting the ball through one of six small, ball-shaped holes.

Still, many aspects of Cuju sound amazingly modern. During the Tang dynasty (A.D. 618 to 907), Cuju balls were filled with air instead of feathers and the game became even more popular. Not only emperors, but many rich citizens began to build their own Cuju fields and form professional teams. Some would entertain the emperor, but other teams traveled around playing teams in other large cities—just like professional players do today.

In the beginning, Cuju was played only by men, but more than 1,000 years ago, women began playing it, too. Stories from the Song dynasty (around the 10th century) describe a game involving 153 women! They were dressed in colorful uniforms or embroidered silk and played in front of an audience of tens of thousands of people.

By modern times, Cuju was no longer played in China, but a form of it still exists in Japan. Because of its military history, Cuju was always considered a violent game, but it took on a very different form when it was introduced to Japan around A.D. 644. Called Kemari, this game is not competitive, but cooperative. The object is for a team of players to try and keep a ball in the air as long as they can using anything except their arms and hands. Today, Kemari is played mainly as part of religious festivals in Japan.

KEMARI GAME

Sports in Ancient Egypt

Though the games clearly have a lot of similarities, many modern experts and historians doubt that there is any real link between Cuju and modern soccer. They point out that many ancient civilizations had their own types of ball games, and that some of those were pretty close to soccer, too.

Art is the main way for people today to know about the sports of ancient Egypt. From scenes depicted on the walls of pyramids and temples, it's obvious that sports and fitness were important aspects of life in ancient Egypt. Paintings show people competing at gymnastics and archery and many other types of sports. Stories written down on scrolls made from papyrus (an ancient form of paper) also give accounts of some of these games.

EGYPTIAN MURAL DEPICTING WRESTLING

Balls made of linen (a type of cloth) or animal skins have been found in Egyptian tombs that date back to 2,500 B.C. Based on drawings from those times, experts believe the people of Egypt played a game similar to soccer at special festivals. They wrapped up balls in bright-colored cloth and kicked them across the ground to celebrate the many things that grew from the earth. Still, when people today think of sports in the ancient world, they are more likely to think of Greece than Egypt.

Greeks and Romans

Sports were very important to the ancient Greeks. The first Olympics were held in Greece in 776 B.C. These Games continued for more than 12 centuries until A.D. 393. Even in times of war, a truce would be called so that the sports competitions could take place in peace.

While the Olympics set a new standard for spectator sports in the ancient world, it seems that all of the sports and games there were just for individual athletes. But outside the Olympics in ancient Greece, there were team sports. Some of these sports wouldn't seem very organized to us today. They were more like playground or school yard games, such as dodgeball, in which these ancient competitors mainly threw balls at each other. The Greeks also played a game called *episkyros*. It was mostly played by men, but women played it, too. Episkyros is listed among the ancient forms of European football (soccer), but it sounds like the game was much closer to an ancient version of North American football.

Teams in episkyros usually were made up of 12 to 14 players, and these players would try to kick or throw a ball over the heads of their opponents and across a goal line. Episkyros may even have included ancient aspects of baseball or hockey, because some sources say the ball could be hit with a stick, too. One thing that's known for sure about episkyros is that—like most Greek sports—it was usually played in the nude!

The Greeks had another ball game they called *harpaston*. When it's described, it doesn't sound much different from episkyros. It seems to have been another game where the object was to run, throw, or kick a ball across a goal line. Again it sounds a lot like North American

A PAINTING SHOWING HARPASTUM FROM FIRST-CENTURY A.D. ROME

HARPASTUM GAME

football, and it was said to be a very rough game. The strange thing is, the word harpaston in Greek actually means "handball," so it's kind of hard to say for sure that there's any real link to modern soccer ... but the Greeks certainly kept the ball rolling!

By about 100 B.C., Rome was the largest city in the world, and the Roman Empire would soon spread across much of what is now Europe, Africa, and Asia today. The Romans had their own version of episkyros and harpaston that they called *harpastum*. To Romans, harpastum was known as "the small ball game" because it was played with a ball that was about the size of a grapefruit. It may have been small, but it would probably have hurt to be hit with the ball, since it was made of leather and stuffed full of sand. Harpastum was played on a rectangular field with boundary lines at the sides and ends and a center line across the middle. It was probably played by teams of five to 12 players. Like the Greek game, this Roman sport may actually have been more like American football than soccer, since both throwing and kicking the ball were allowed, but it had one big difference from either of our modern games: The object of harpastum was not to score in a net or get the ball across a goal line. By passing the ball from player to player, the idea

A BRONZE STATUE OF A ROMAN CHARIOT

THE WORLD'S OLDEST SOCCER BALL

As far back as Roman times, balls for sports were being made from the bladders of pigs. Blowing air into these bladders like balloons couldn't have been a very fun job, but there was probably some sort of clay pipe so that people didn't have to put their mouths directly onto these animal innards!

The biggest problem with using a pig's bladder is that—like a balloon—once they were blown up with air, they would sometimes pop. So people started to sew leather covers made from animal skins over the top of the bladders. Today, the oldest soccer ball in the world can be found in a museum in Stirling, Scotland. It was found in the rafters above a bedroom in Stirling Castle. The ball probably belonged to Mary, Queen of Scots, when she was a little girl in the 1500s. The ball is made from a pig's bladder wrapped in cow leather and is likely more than 450 years old.

Diaries kept by Mary when she was a girl prove that she played soccer and golf. It's believed that when she was queen, Mary would throw a ball from her balcony at the start of games between her soldiers and her royal servants. This ball from her bedroom could be one of those.

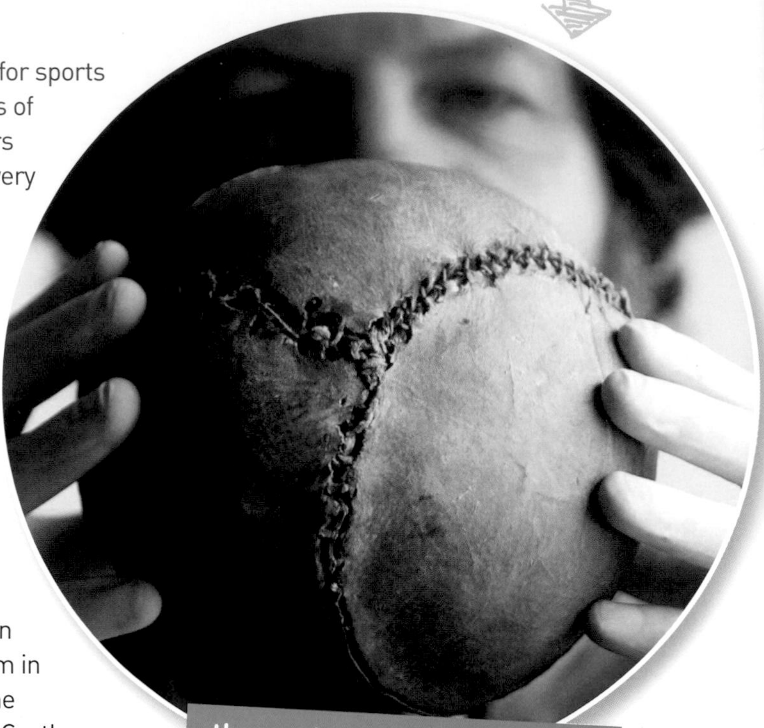

the world's oldest soccer ball in Stirling, Scotland

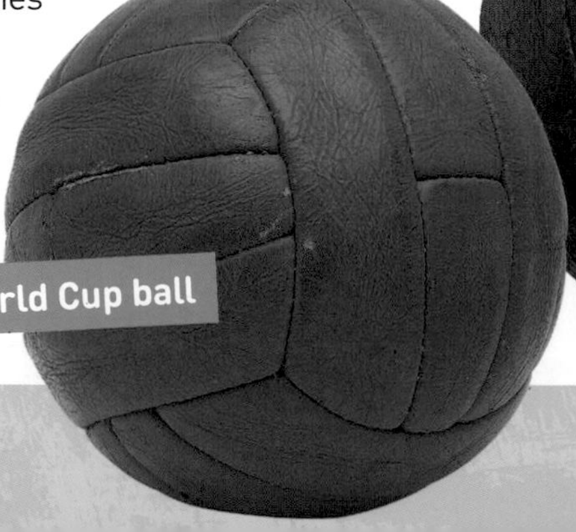

1966 World Cup ball

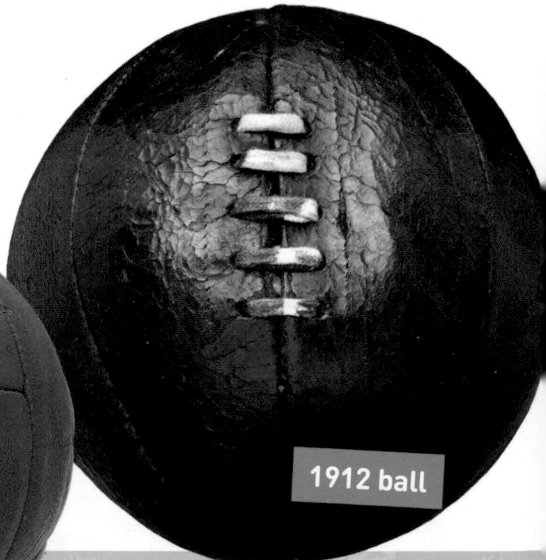

1912 ball

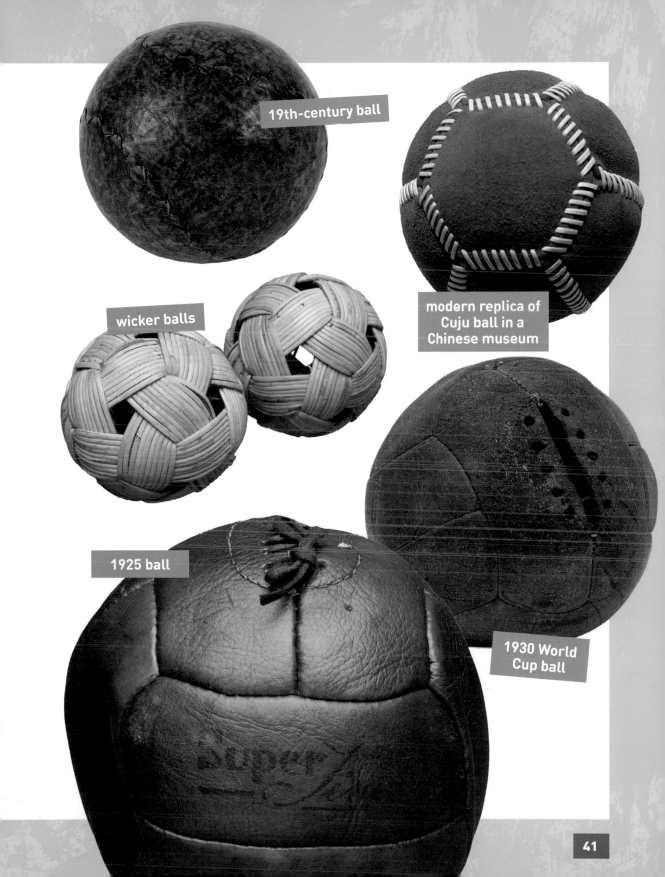

19th-century ball

modern replica of Cuju ball in a Chinese museum

wicker balls

1925 ball

1930 World Cup ball

was for each team to keep the ball in the air for as long as they could while keeping it on their own side of the center line. Meanwhile, the other team was trying to steal the ball and bring it back to their side of the line. It appears that points were scored whenever the ball hit the ground, so it would seem likely that the lowest score won the game.

Each player on a harpastum team had his own specific role to play. There must have been lots of special tactics designed to get players into the open, but there doesn't appear to have been any blockers like there are in football. As in soccer, only the player with the ball could be tackled. A man known as Galen was a Greek doctor and philosopher who lived in Rome before A.D. 200. He was a big fan of harpastum and once wrote that the game "entails no danger." Still, even Galen had to admit that the rules about contact weren't always followed very closely. "When people face each other, vigorously attempting to prevent each other from taking the space between, [it can involve] much use

of the hold by the neck, and many wrestling holds."

The Roman Empire ruled over what is now England for almost 400 years from A.D. 43 to 410. It's believed that the Romans brought harpastum with them to England during this time. This has probably led to the many legends all across Britain that the Romans introduced soccer to their country. There are records of games of harpastum being played between the Romans and the natives of Britain, but there's really no proof this had anything at all to do with the development of modern soccer.

So, how did the game we know today as soccer really get started?

English Soccer in the Middle Ages

The time in European history known as the Middle Ages or the Medieval Period lasted from the fifth century to the 15th century. This was about 600 to 1,600 years ago. The Middle Ages have long been thought of as a dark time in

ANCIENT SPORTS CLOSER TO HOME

The people of China, Africa, and Europe weren't the only ones playing ball games in ancient times. There were games in Mesoamerica too. This was a region stretching south from about the middle of Mexico through several countries in what is now known as Central America. The Mesoamericans had a game that seems to be a blend of what is now soccer, basketball, and football. It featured a ball wrapped in rubber made from tree sap that had to be knocked through a hoop or into a goal. Players knocked the ball around with their hips, although some versions of the rules may have allowed arms, bats, or racquets. A hip game similar to soccer is still played in some parts of Mexico today. It's known as Ulama.

PLAYING ULAMA IN MODERN MEXICO

AN EARLY ITALIAN GAME CALLED *CALCIO*

Western human history. Modern scholars now believe this is too simple a view, but it is true that much of the science and art that flourished during the Greek and Roman Empires was forgotten. The Middle Ages were a time of warfare and dreaded diseases. Unless you were a king or queen, or a member of a wealthy, noble family, life could be very hard indeed.

Many countries that today are part of modern Europe have legends about soccer-type games that date back to the Middle Ages. Just as in England, many claim that the games were originally introduced as the Roman game of harpastum, but it's hard to prove that. Some stories claim that the Vikings invented soccer by kicking around the chopped-off heads of their enemies. Pretty gross!

Viking invaders from Denmark attacked England many times during the years from A.D. 793 to 1066, which leads to one of the most famous legends about how soccer began—and it's pretty gross, too! According to these stories, after a Danish occupation of England ended around 1042, English workers plowing their fields would often come across the bodies of dead Viking soldiers. Whenever they dug them up, they would make a game out of kicking around their skulls. But there's no good proof that the stories are real.

Still, it may be true that the Vikings introduced soccer to England, and it doesn't have anything to do with dead bodies. There are written accounts of Viking games in several of the

KEEPING THE BALL ROLLING

MARK GEIGER

Although these ancient games may only have a slight resemblance to the modern game of soccer, there are many aspects of these early sports that we can see being used on the practice field today. For example, when young kids start to learn about playing positions, a coach may allow them to throw the ball instead of kicking. This can keep the game moving faster, which helps the kids learn to adjust their position to each new situation. We see many smaller games of 2v2, 3v3, or 5v5 ("keep away") to help develop skills in keeping possession of the ball in tight spaces. Players also practice their skills individually by juggling the ball, keeping the ball in the air as long as they can to help develop their touch on the ball. So, even though these ancient games have mostly disappeared, many of their aspects can be found on the practice field in present-day soccer.

A NORTH AMERICAN GAME

A PAINTING OF ANCIENT LACROSSE DATING FROM THE 1840s

Native Americans and the First Nations people of Canada are well known for playing a game like lacrosse. It was known by many different names depending on who was playing it, but it's best known as baggataway, which means "little brother of war." The game was often used for settling disputes, and though it could be very violent it was much better than a real war. A game played by the Algonquian tribe was known as *pasuckuako-howog*, meaning "they gather to play ball with the foot." It was a lot like mob football, though the early European settlers were surprised by how much less brutal this game was. One description from 1612 reads: "they never strike up one another's heeles, as we do."

Nordic sagas (tales of the ancient people of Denmark, Norway, Sweden, and Iceland). The games had names like *knattleikr, soppleik,* and *skofuleik*. Unfortunately, it seems that whoever wrote these sagas assumed that their readers already knew about these games so they don't really explain how they were played. Based on what has been written, it seems that they may have been like some sort of combination of football and baseball or hockey, since players could run with the ball and use a stick to hit it—and, sometimes, to hit each other.

So did soccer in England really develop from games the British people learned from the Vikings? Maybe,

but maybe not. Unfortunately, it's impossible to know for sure when any of these soccer-like games were first played in England.

Mob Football

Have you ever been to a big professional sporting event or watched one on television? For professional American football, Super Bowl Sunday is practically a national holiday in the United States. College bowl games on New Year's Day have been an American tradition for more than 100 years. The National Hockey League's annual Winter Classic game, played outdoors in football or baseball stadiums, has become a new

CHEERING AT A MODERN AMERICAN FOOTBALL GAME

A PAINTING FROM ITALY IN THE 1500s

GAMES WERE OFTEN PLAYED BETWEEN NEIGHBORING TOWNS AND VILLAGES AND FEATURED **UNLIMITED PLAYERS**

tradition on January 1. Baseball's Toronto Blue Jays always fill the stadium when they're at home on Canada Day on July 1, and teams across the United States also expect big crowds on the Fourth of July. But imagine if these huge crowds weren't just cheering from the stands. What would it be like if all those fans were actually out there on the field playing the game? That's what soccer was like in England and France in the Middle Ages.

Soccer from the Middle Ages is often referred to now as medieval football. Sometimes it's called Shrovetide football because it was a tradition to play it on the holiday of Shrove Tuesday. Other more colorful names for the game are folk football and mob football. It certainly must have been a mob scene! These games were often played between neighboring towns and villages, and they featured unlimited numbers of players on each team.

SOCCER IN SHAKESPEARE

SOCCER HAD BECOME SO POPULAR IN ENGLAND that William Shakespeare mentioned the game, as football, in two of his plays. Shakespeare wrote *The Comedy of Errors* around 1594. In Act 2, Scene 1, a character says:

Am I so round with you as you with me,
That like a football you do spurn me thus?
You spurn me hence, and he will spurn me hither.
If I last in this service, you must case me in leather.

In another play, *King Lear*, which was first performed in 1606, Shakespeare has one character insult another by calling him a "base football player."

Games weren't played on special fields but often right through the streets of the towns. Players were allowed to kick, throw, or run with the ball. Sometimes there were goalposts set up at the edge of a town, but often the object was to force the ball into the village square at the center of the opposing town. Other times, the goal was to kick the ball into the balcony of the opponent's church.

These days, people often refer to soccer as "The Beautiful Game," but there was nothing pretty about mob football. It may have been fun to play if you were big and strong, but it was probably a little bit scary to be caught up in the surging mass of players. Sometimes, people were even killed. Even when people didn't get killed, mob football games resulted in a lot of injuries. With such large gangs of players filling the streets, it was also hard for shopkeepers to go about their business. More than 700 years ago, the merchants of London complained to their mayor about this. It led to a proclamation from King Edward II on April 13, 1314, that banned soccer. Anyone caught playing could be imprisoned. Several other kings also banned

soccer during the 1300s and the 1400s.

Even so, these soccer-like games were always so popular among the people of England that they kept bouncing back. Bans against mob football never lasted for long. They may even have made the game more popular—but it always remained dangerous.

The Game Starts to Take Shape

By the beginning of the 1600s, people were starting to play soccer in a way that would begin to look more like what we watch and play today. Writers from that time have described a game where the ball is passed from player to player and where the object is to score a goal. When it comes to soccer and other early sports, the most important book of the 17th century is Francis Willughby's *Book of Plaies (Book of Games)*, which was written during the 1660s.

A friend once described Willughby as having been "bitten by the snake of knowledge." Willughby's main interests were insects, birds, and fish, but lucky for us he was a sports fan,

A GAME IN ENGLAND PAINTED IN 1827

PLAYING IN THE PHILIPPINES AROUND 1845

too. His book covers all sorts of games and pastimes including card games and children's games, as well as sports such as tennis and others that were clearly early forms of baseball. Sadly, Willughby wasn't finished working on his book when he died in 1672, but what he did write is pretty amazing. The book was held for more than three centuries in a collection at the University of Nottingham in England before a modern edition was finally published in 2003.

A DEPICTION OF SOCCER FROM THE LATE 1800s

When it comes to soccer, Willughby describes a game that had come a long way from mob football. He writes that players had to kick the ball toward the other team's goal and were not allowed to carry or throw it. He talks about teams that were "equally divided according to their strength and nimbleness." Willughby doesn't specifically mention positions, but it's pretty easy to see from his description that some of the players were more responsible for scoring goals than others who were trying to stop them. "They usually leave some of their best players to guard the goal," Willughby says.

Soccer in England was clearly a game popular among all people, from the common folk to the highest levels of the upper class. That's still true today. Yet, upper-class English schools for the children of wealthy and important families (called private schools in North America, but they're known as public schools in England) had a very big role in changing the way that soccer was played.

The earliest stories about soccer at a public school in England go all the way back to Winchester College in 1640. That's almost 400 years ago. People there described the game as "innocent and lawful." But even if people had begun to play soccer the way Francis Willughby described it, some of the roughness of mob

A GAME IN ITALY IN THE 1700s

18TH CENTURY

AN ITALIAN NOBLEMAN PLAYING SOCCER

A BOY IN HIS FOOTBALL KIT IN 1910

20TH CENTURY

healthy mind. They thought sports and exercise would be a good way to keep people out of trouble. Even at Shrewsbury School, when Benjamin Kennedy became the new headmaster in 1836, soccer became an important part of student life. In fact, the kids at Shrewsbury were forced to play soccer three times a week, whether they liked it or not.

Other schools may not have forced their students to play soccer, but many headmasters shared the same enthusiasm for sports and exercise. Still, there was a bit of a problem when it came to soccer. There were no set rules. Every school seemed to come up with its own unique way to play the game. The rules they invented would depend on such things as the size of the balls they had, the size of the field they could play on, and the type of goalposts they could set up. Oftentimes the rules that developed were so complicated and peculiar that anybody watching who didn't go to that school would have a hard time figuring out what was going on. (Even if they play soccer today, some of the old English public schools continue to play their own old-fashioned games as well.) And violence was still a problem, too. At the very least, people often kicked their opponents in the shins on purpose. At the worst, some of the games these schools played didn't seem much more civilized than mob football.

A Different Type of Football

The public school in the town of Rugby, in the English county of Warwickshire, was established in 1567. You may have heard the word "rugby" before. Maybe you've even played the game of rugby, or watched others play it. Well, the sport of rugby got its start at Rugby School—and it was started by a frustrated soccer player who wasn't happy using only his feet.

football still remained for many years. Samuel Butler became the headmaster at Shrewsbury School in 1798, and he obviously didn't have a very high opinion of soccer. He once described it as being "more fit for farm boys and labourers than young gentlemen." However, most other public schools in England were happy to let their students play soccer.

By the 1800s, people were beginning to believe that a healthy body helped make a

RUGBY WAS STARTED BY A FRUSTRATED SOCCER PLAYER WHO WASN'T HAPPY USING ONLY HIS FEET.

RUGBY FOOTBALL IN ENGLAND IN 1882

SOCCER – RUGBY – FOOTBALL

American football in Canada and the United States started with the game of rugby. By the early 1870s, rugby was becoming a popular sport at some Canadian universities. At McGill University in Montreal, students played with an oval rugby ball they could pick up and run with whenever they liked. At Harvard University near Boston, Massachusetts, U.S.A., students played a game with a round soccer ball. Theirs was mostly a kicking game, but if a player was being chased, he was allowed to pick up the ball and run with it or even throw it. On May 14 and 15, 1874, a team from McGill visited Harvard for a two-game series. The first game was played with American rules, but the second was played with Canadian rules. Harvard players liked the Canadian rugby rules better, and they soon introduced them to other American universities. That's how American football got started.

Rugby School had purchased a field in 1784 for its young students to play on. They were certainly playing soccer on it by the early years of the 1800s, but the soccer played at Rugby School was pretty different from today's game. Matthew Bloxam was born in 1805 and lived his whole life in the town of Rugby. His father helped run the school, and Bloxam was a student there between 1813 and 1820. Many years later, he wrote a letter that described the type of soccer played at the school in his day. Every student was expected to play, and the teams could have more than 100 players on each side. "Few and simple were the rules of the game," wrote Bloxam. "[N]o one was allowed to run with the ball in his grasp towards the opposite goal. It was football and not handball."

In another letter he wrote in 1880, Bloxam described how the game of rugby got its start at

AN 1879 BRITISH MAGAZINE COVER SHOWING A GAME OF RUGBY AT RUGBY SCHOOL

Rugby School. It all began in 1823 when a boy named William Webb Ellis caught the ball in his arms while playing soccer. Ellis wasn't the goalie, but it wasn't against the rules of soccer at Rugby for any player to catch the ball. What should have happened next was that Ellis would get a free kick. No one on the other team could rush at him until he had punted the ball, or placed it

on the field for someone else on his team to kick. But instead of doing that, as soon as Ellis caught the ball, he began running with it in his arms toward the opponent's goal. Other students at Rugby liked the idea and the game caught on. On August 28, 1845, the rules were written down for the first time as the Laws of Football Played at Rugby School. After that, anybody who wanted to play rugby knew how they were supposed to do it.

It all seems pretty simple, but is the story told by Matthew Bloxam really true? It's impossible to know for sure. William Webb Ellis never seems to have told anybody about it himself. He was already dead when Bloxam wrote his letters, so nobody could ask him. Bloxam himself was dead, too, when a few old members of Rugby School decided to investigate the story in 1895. They interviewed the few men they could find who were old enough to remember. These men remembered that the game at Rugby had once been a lot like soccer. Then, sometime between 1820 and 1830, players had started to run with the ball. However, these men believed that running with the ball was still considered against the rules until sometime between 1830 and 1840. So, could Ellis have been the first one to run with the ball? Nobody knew if that was true, but one man said that he remembered Ellis as being someone who was "generally regarded as inclined to take unfair advantages at football." There really wasn't any proof, but the investigators decided to stick with the story and commissioned a special plaque that still exists as part of a wall at Rugby School.

THIS STONE
COMMEMORATES THE EXPLOIT OF
WILLIAM WEBB ELLIS
WHO WITH A FINE DISREGARD FOR THE RULES OF FOOTBALL
AS PLAYED IN HIS TIME
FIRST TOOK THE BALL IN HIS ARMS AND RAN WITH IT
THUS ORIGINATING THE DISTINCTIVE FEATURE OF
THE RUGBY GAME
A.D. 1823
PRESENTED BY RUGBY SCHOOL
24TH FEBRUARY 1972

THE FIRST RUGBY PLAYER
In appreciation
THE RUGBY FOOTBALL UNION

A STONE AT THE GRAVE OF WILLIAM WEBB ELLIS

FIELD REPORT

OVER THE CENTURIES, soccer has evolved a great deal into the sport that we play or watch on our local fields and on television today. However, we only need to have watched games over the last few decades to see how much the game is still changing. Even though there have only been minor changes to the rules of the game in recent years, the styles of play, the tactics, the speed, skill, and overall athleticism have changed and improved dramatically. In the early years of the modern game, soccer was seen as a gentleman's sport. The referee took a position off the field, wore a suit, and would only make a ruling if the players on each team had a dispute they couldn't resolve by themselves. Now, the players are so much faster and stronger, so the game moves much faster, too. Even the referees have to train like players so they can be in the right position with the right angle to make a decision about a particular play. I think it will be very interesting to see where this game will be In another 20 years.

MARK GEIGER

A SOCCER MATCH IN ENGLAND IN 1909

THE TEAM CAPTAINS FOR GERMANY AND SPAIN JOIN THE REFEREE TO CHOOSE SIDES OF THE FIELD FOR THE 1942 GAME IN BERLIN'S OLYMPIC STADIUM.

GET IN THE GAME

WHEN DOES A SPORT BECOME A SPORT?

Is it enough just to be a fun activity that people like to do? Or do you need official rules? There aren't a lot of team sports where we can say for sure exactly how or when they started. Basketball is one of them. It was invented by Canadian James Naismith in 1891 when he worked at a YMCA school in Springfield, Massachusetts, U.S.A. Naismith was asked to come up with a safe, new sport to be played indoors in winter. He based his original 13 rules for basketball on a stone-throwing game he'd played as a child. But even Naismith's brand new sport had similarities to an ancient Mesoamerican game.

In her Harry Potter books, author J.K. Rowling invented a sport called Quidditch. It's played by wizards on magic broomsticks, but fans of the books liked the sport so much, they figured out a way to play it on fields without having to fly!

If you were to invent a new team sport, how would you do it? Take a look at these five questions on the opposite page to get you thinking, and then grab a ball, a puck, or whatever equipment you need, and some friends, and get playing!

UNIVERSITY STUDENTS PLAY QUIDDITCH IN KINGSTON, ONTARIO, CANADA.

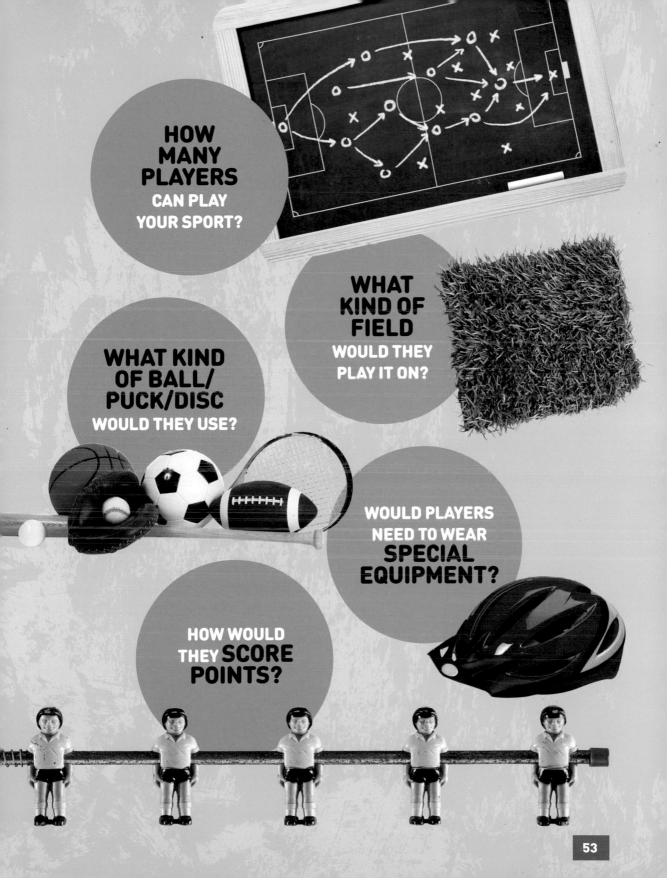

HOW MANY PLAYERS CAN PLAY YOUR SPORT?

WHAT KIND OF FIELD WOULD THEY PLAY IT ON?

WHAT KIND OF BALL/PUCK/DISC WOULD THEY USE?

WOULD PLAYERS NEED TO WEAR SPECIAL EQUIPMENT?

HOW WOULD THEY SCORE POINTS?

FACES FROM ALL 32 NATIONS AT THE 2014 WORLD CUP IN BRAZIL

CHAPTER 3

SOCCER AROUND THE WORLD

INTRODUCTION

SOCCER IS THE WORLD'S GAME.

In the United States and Canada, you see kids playing football, baseball, basketball, and hockey in streets and parks. Outside of North America, you almost only see soccer. Kids around the world grow up worshipping their favorite soccer teams, and players like Lionel Messi from Argentina, Marta Vieira da Silva from Brazil, and Cristiano Ronaldo from Portugal inspire young people to become better players, maybe even to become stars themselves.

MARK GEIGER

You only need to look at the number of international tournaments and competitions sponsored by FIFA and its confederations to see how big soccer is around the world. The crown jewels are the FIFA World Cup and the FIFA Women's World Cup, which are held every four years.

Additionally, FIFA holds a men's and women's Under-20 (U-20) and Under-17 (U-17) World Cup every two years. It also holds the FIFA Club World Cup every year to crown the best professional team in the world.

Soccer is organized into six confederations—or zones—throughout the world. (You'll learn a little more about these later in this chapter on pages 76–77.) Within each confederation, there are between 10 and 55 different national teams. When you add in all these regional tournaments and competitions, the sport's popularity is clear.

In my career as a referee, I've been very fortunate to have worked at several of these FIFA tournaments, as well as the Olympic Games. In 2011, I worked at the FIFA U-20 World Cup in Colombia. In 2012, I worked at the Olympic Games in London. In 2013, I worked at the FIFA Club World Cup in Morocco. Finally, in 2014, I worked at the FIFA World Cup in Brazil. To be able to experience the culture of each of these different countries was amazing—and to experience it during a world tournament takes it to a whole different level! Everywhere I traveled, I found people proud to show me their city and their soccer traditions.

All the stadiums in which I worked were huge. They were very similar to the football stadiums that I see in the United States. They were packed with people screaming and cheering for their national teams and heroes. From the field, the sea of colors in the stands and on the pitch is a sight and an experience I will never forget. Soccer truly is the world's game, and I am thankful to have the opportunity to feel the passion and love from all around the globe.

GERMAN PLAYERS CELEBRATE THEIR VICTORY AT THE 2007 WOMEN'S WORLD CUP.

SOCCER IS TRULY **THE** WORLD'S GAME.

NEYMAR LED BRAZIL TO THE GOLD MEDAL OVER GERMANY AT THE 2016 OLYMPICS IN RIO DE JANEIRO.

NEYMAR

MANY COUNTRIES IN EUROPE AND OTHER PARTS OF THE WORLD ALREADY HAD TRADITIONAL SOCCER-TYPE GAMES, but it was only after the official rules were established in Britain by the Football Association that soccer really began to spread.

The game of soccer traveled from person to person across the globe. Individuals wanted to bring their love of the game with them and play it wherever they went. Soon the game was being played all around the world.

Rule Britannia

By the 1880s, many English soccer teams had begun to pay salaries to their best players. This was especially important in the northern part of England, where there tended to be more working-class players than in the south. In the wealthy, upper-class families of London and other parts of southern England, players didn't have to worry so much about making a living. In the north, it could be hard to convince the best players to join teams if it meant time away from their jobs.

The Football Association agreed to allow professional players—players who were paid—in the summer of 1885. This helped pave the way for England's first football league, which was formed in 1888. The Football Association is still the main governing body for soccer in England to this day. The English Football League (EFL), which was formed in 1888, was the top soccer league in England until 1992. That year, the top 22 clubs in the EFL broke away to form the

MANCHESTER UNITED VERSUS SOUTHAMPTON IN 2016

ENGLISH WOMEN IN THE EARLY 1900s

Premier League, which remains the top league. The EFL is now sort of like the minor leagues in baseball or hockey, except that EFL teams are not farm teams to the Premier League teams. They all act independently and can even reach the Premier League if they win their league championship.

Many of the top English soccer teams have fans all over the world. Perhaps the most famous team is Manchester United from the northern part of England. The club was formed in 1878 as Newton Heath LYR Football Club and has been known by its current name since 1902. Manchester United has won a record 20 league championships and has won the FA Cup a record-tying 12 times.

The United Kingdom (which has been made up of England, Scotland, Wales, and Northern Ireland since 1801) didn't just invent the modern rules of soccer during the 1800s. The UK actually ruled much of the world at that time! In fact, England, and later the UK, was the most

STATUES OUTSIDE OLD TRAFFORD

OLD TRAFFORD

MANCHESTER UNITED HAS PLAYED ITS GAMES on the same site for more than 100 years. Old Trafford stadium has been its home since February 19, 1910. It was almost destroyed by a German bombing raid during World War II on March 11, 1941. For the next eight years, Manchester United had to share a stadium with its crosstown rival, Manchester City, before Old Trafford finally reopened on August 24, 1949.

Today, the stands at Old Trafford are named after two of Manchester United's greatest legends. The south stands are named for Sir Bobby Charlton, who led England to its only World Cup title, in 1966. The north stands are named in honor of Sir Alex Ferguson, who was the manager at "Man U" from 1986 to 2013. During that time, Ferguson led the team to 13 Premier League championships and five FA Cup titles.

ZLATAN IBRAHIMOVIĆ SCORES FOR MAN U.

THE NEWTON HEATH LYR FOOTBALL CLUB IN 1892

AN EARLY SOCCER GAME IN GERMANY

SOLEIL DU DIMANCHE
A FRENCH NEWSPAPER FROM 1902

A PHOTOGRAPH OF GERMAN SOCCER FROM 1905

powerful country in the world for about 400 years, from the mid-1500s until the mid-1900s.

Even in countries that had never been controlled by England, the English usually had plenty of influence. Often it was because of its army or navy, but it was also because of British companies that did business all around the world. As British citizens traveled near and far between the 1860s and 1890s, they often took their sports with them. Here's how soccer got its start in some of the countries around the world that play it best today.

How Soccer Spread

Stories about football in France go back even further in history than they do in England. The oldest known reference to a French ball game was written by the Bishop of Clermont around 470. That game was probably something very similar to the games played in ancient Greece and Rome.

Many experts believe there is probably a link between the medieval soccer games played in England and France dating back to 1066. That's when England was invaded by the Normans, who came from Normandy in what is now the northern part of France. Unfortunately, even if there is a connection, it's impossible to say which country might have introduced the game to the other. Whichever way it went, it's pretty clear that a game like soccer was being played in France by the late 1300s. However, this game would have been a lot more like mob football in England than it was like modern soccer.

Modern soccer was introduced to France in 1872 by English sailors playing in the port city of Le Havre.

Today, the top soccer league in France is known as the Ligue de Football Professionnel. It was founded in 1944. Its top two divisions are known simply as Ligue 1 and Ligue 2. The best 20 teams in France play in Ligue 1. There are also 20 clubs in Ligue 2. Saint-Etienne, Marseille, and Paris Saint-Germain are among the most popular and successful teams in France today.

Modern soccer was brought to Italy during the 1880s. There are different stories about how it might have happened. One is the story of a young Italian man named Edoardo Bosio. Bosio was born in Turin, Italy, in 1864. He later worked for a British company that made cloth and other fabrics, and he had the opportunity to live in London for a while. Bosio became a big fan of soccer, and when he returned home to Turin in 1886, he brought his love of the game with him. In 1887, he founded the Torino Football and Cricket Club. Soccer was quick to catch on in Italy, with leagues and a governing body set up by 1898. Today, Italy has a complicated system of leagues that involve nearly 600 divisions and over 3,000 teams. The top league is known as Serie A and features the country's 20 best teams. Among the most popular teams in Italy, and all around the world, are Juventus, based in Turin, and A.C. Milan and Inter Milan, who both play in the city of Milan.

The first true soccer team in Germany was formed in 1874 by Englishmen living and working in Dresden. They called it the Dresden English Football Club. The club had more than 70 members, who played games watched by hundreds of fans.

By the end of the 1890s, Germany was beginning to look at England as a major rival in world affairs. Soccer was already becoming very popular, but many Germans didn't like the idea that it was an English game.

CRISTIANO RONALDO

IN 2015, CRISTIANO RONALDO was named the best Portuguese player of all time by the Portuguese Football Federation during its 100th anniversary celebration. He's played for Portugal at the World Cup in 2006, 2010, and 2014 and led his country to the UEFA European Championship title (known as the Euro) in 2016. Back in 2002–03, Ronaldo led Sporting CP to a 3–1 win over Manchester United. Man U was so impressed that it signed him to a contract. The transfer fee of 12.4 million British pounds was the most ever paid for a teenage player. Since 2009, Ronaldo has played in Spain with Real Madrid, where he has battled with Lionel Messi of FC Barcelona in a great rivalry for league titles and scoring championships, as well as to see who is the best player in soccer today.

CRISTIANO RONALDO

RONALDO WAS NAMED THE BEST PORTUGUESE PLAYER OF ALL TIME BY THE PORTUGUESE FOOTBALL FEDERATION.

LIONEL MESSI

MANY FANS AND SOCCER EXPERTS consider Lionel Messi to be the greatest player in the world today. Some even think he's the greatest of all time. Messi was born in Argentina but has spent most of his career in Spain playing for FC Barcelona. Messi has set La Liga records for most goals in a single season and the most goals in a career, and he has also scored more goals for Argentina's national team than any other player in history. When he briefly decided to retire during the summer of 2016, even the president of Argentina urged him not to. "It is one of life's pleasures, it is a gift from God to have the best player in the world in a footballing country like ours," said the president. "Lionel Messi is the greatest thing we have in Argentina and we must take care of him."

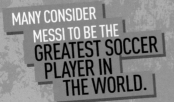

MANY CONSIDER MESSI TO BE THE GREATEST SOCCER PLAYER IN THE WORLD.

LIONEL MESSI

So they tried to promote stories about traditional soccer-style games in their own country. The problem was, there weren't nearly as many stories about such games as there were in places like England, France, and Italy. One of the few German folktales about soccer tells of a kind of ceremonial game played at weddings. That game was known as brautball, which means brideball. Unfortunately, there's almost no information about how it was played.

Today, soccer in Germany has a system with even more divisions and teams than Italy. The top German league is known as the Bundesliga (which means Federal League). It has 18 teams. One of the most famous teams in Germany is Bayern Munich, which has won more league titles and national cups than any other team in Germany.

Students from Portugal who were studying in England were the first to bring soccer to their country. The first organized game was played on the Portuguese island of Madeira in 1875. Britain had controlled Madeira for a brief time in the early 1800s, helping Portugal to defend it in a war against France. Although this friendly occupation ended in 1814, the relationship between England, Portugal, and Madeira remained a good one. Harry Hinton was the son of a father whose family was English and a mother from Madeira. Hinton was born on the Portuguese island but later went to school in England. He was the one who organized Portugal's first game, in 1875, after bringing a soccer ball home with him.

Today, the top league in Portugal is known as the Primeira Liga. It has 18 teams. The league was first organized in 1934. Its three best

SERGIO RAMOS OF REAL MADRID HEADS THE BALL TO SCORE A GOAL.

FC BARCELONA VERSUS REAL MADRID IN SPAIN'S LA LIGA

clubs—known as the Big Three—are S.L. Benfica and Sporting CP, who are both based in the capital of Lisbon, and FC Porto from the city of Porto. Between them, they have won all but two of the Portuguese championships since the Primeira Liga was formed.

The first soccer team in Spain didn't really start out to play soccer. It began as a way for British workers at a Spanish mine near the city of Huelva to get some fresh air and exercise above the ground. It was set up by two doctors from Scotland just before Christmas, on December 23, 1889. They called their club the Huelva Recreation Club. It still exists as a soccer team today under the Spanish

A POSTCARD OF SEVILLA FC FROM ABOUT 1922

name Real Club Recreativo de Huelva.

Just a few weeks later, on January 25, 1890, in the town of Seville, about 60 miles (97 km) away from Huelva, some British businessmen living there formed the Sevilla Football Club.

The first practice was held at the beginning of February on a field for horse racing, where they set out the boundaries and put up goalposts. More and more players began to show up in the following weeks. Knowing about the club in Huelva, the members of the Sevilla club wrote the Huelva miners a letter and asked them to form their own team and come to Seville for a game.

BRAZILIAN SOCCER LEGEND PELÉ IN ACTION AGAINST BULGARIA IN THE 1966 WORLD CUP

THE GREATEST PLAYER EVER

THE ATHLETE MOST PEOPLE CONSIDER TO BE THE GREATEST PLAYER in soccer history grew up with very little money in Brazil. His name is Edson Arantes do Nascimento, but everyone knows him as Pelé. Taught to play by his father, who had also been a great soccer player, Pelé couldn't afford a soccer ball, so he often had to play using a grapefruit or a sock stuffed with newspapers. Still, he was so good that he signed his first professional contract with Santos FC in 1956 when he was only 15 years old. He made the Brazilian national team when he was 16 and won the World Cup with them for the first time in 1958 when he was 17. In a career that stretched from 1956 to 1977, Pelé is credited with scoring an all-time record 1,281 goals in 1,363 games played.

PELÉ IN THE UNIFORM OF THE NEW YORK COSMOS

Within a few years, British sailors and Spanish citizens who'd gone to school in England had set up other teams in Spain. By 1900, there were enough teams to form a league.

Today, the top league in Spain is known simply as La Liga. Its top level is known as the Primera División. It began with 10 teams in 1929 but has had 20 clubs since 1997. The two best teams in Spain are Real Madrid and FC Barcelona, who have combined to win more than half the championships in the history of La Liga. They are two of the most famous soccer teams in the world. They always pack the stadium when they play each other, with millions more watching on television. Whenever Barcelona faces Real Madrid, their game is known as El Clásico, which means The Classic.

By 1867, there was a large British community living in Argentina. Most people were in the capital city of Buenos Aires. Many of them had come to South America as managers or workers with the British-owned railway companies in Argentina. Like so many other British citizens around the world, they brought their sports with them.

The Buenos Aires Cricket Club Ground opened in 1864. Three years later, on June 20, 1867, the first soccer game in Argentina was played at the cricket club. Soccer quickly became a popular game among the British citizens and other European immigrants in Argentina. A league was set up in

1891, followed by another one in 1893 that still exists. But, sadly, the teams in these leagues didn't allow the local citizens to play with them. It wasn't until 1899 that a group of high school students established the first team for Argentine players. It was called Argentino de Quilmes, and it also still exists.

In Argentina today, there are about 450 soccer teams playing in eight different divisions of the Argentine Football Association. The top level is known as the Primera División and has 30 teams. Argentina has produced some of the greatest players in soccer history, but most of the top players from Argentina play for club teams in Europe.

In Brazil, soccer was introduced by Thomas Donohoe, who came from Busby, Scotland, and moved to Rio de Janeiro in 1893. He worked as a dye expert in a textile factory. Donohoe had been an excellent soccer player in Scotland and was

PRIMERA DIVISIÓN
ACTION IN ARGENTINA

WORLD CUP BY THE NUMBERS

YEAR	WINNER	SCORE	RUNNER-UP	HOST COUNTRY	COUNTRIES	GAMES
1930	Uruguay	4–2	Argentina	Uruguay	13	18
1934	Italy	2–1	Czechoslovakia	Italy	16	17
1938	Italy	4–2	Hungary	France	15	18
1950	Uruguay	•	•	Brazil	13	22
1954	West Germany	3–2	Hungary	Switzerland	16	26
1958	Brazil	5–2	Sweden	Sweden	16	35
1962	Brazil	3–1	Czechoslovakia	Chile	16	32
1966	England	4–2 (OT)	West Germany	England	16	32
1970	Brazil	4–1	Italy	Mexico	16	32
1974	West Germany	2–1	Netherlands	West Germany	16	38
1978	Argentina	3–1 (OT)	Netherlands	Argentina	16	38
1982	Italy	3–1	West Germany	Spain	24	52
1986	Argentina	3–1 (OT)	West Germany	Mexico	24	52
1990	West Germany	1–0	Argentina	Italy	24	52
1994	Brazil	0–0*	Italy	United States	24	52
1998	France	3–0	Brazil	France	32	64
2002	Brazil	2–0	Germany	Japan	32	64
2006	Italy	1–1°	France	Germany	32	64
2010	Spain	1–0 (OT)	Netherlands	South Africa	32	64
2014	Germany	1–0 (OT)	Argentina	Brazil	32	64

• Final was played as a four-team round-robin tournament   * Brazil won 3–2 on penalty kicks   ° Italy won 5–3 on penalty kicks

RESULTS BY NATION

TEAM	WINS	RUNNER-UP	TEAM	WINS	RUNNER-UP
Brazil	5	2	England	1	0
Germany	4	4	Spain	1	0
Italy	4	2	Netherlands	0	3
Argentina	2	2	Czechoslovakia	0	2
Uruguay	2	0	Hungary	0	2
France	1	1	Sweden	0	1

GEOFF HURST
of England is the only
player to score a
HAT TRICK
in the Final game
(1966).

BRAZIL is the
only country to
qualify for
**EVERY
WORLD CUP.**

TO DATE, ONLY 50 HAT TRICKS
(THREE GOALS BY ONE PLAYER) HAVE EVER
BEEN SCORED IN OVER 700 WORLD CUP GAMES.

**GABRIEL
BATISTUTA**
of Argentina is the
only player to score a
HAT TRICK
at two World Cups
(1994, 1998).

Only **THREE PLAYERS**
have ever scored
TWO HAT TRICKS
in one World Cup:
Sándor Kocsis, Hungary (1954),
Just Fontaine, France (1958),
Gerd Müller, Germany (1974).

GABRIEL BATISTUTA

JUST FONTAINE

PELÉ (Brazil)
is the only player to
**WIN THE
WORLD CUP
THREE TIMES**
(1958, 1962, 1970).

anxious to start a team when he arrived in Rio. But he couldn't even find a soccer ball in Brazil. Donohoe wrote home to ask for a ball and a pair of shoes. When they arrived, he staked out the boundaries for a soccer pitch near the factory where he worked in the neighborhood of Bangu. Then Donohoe went to other workers' homes trying to find players. He convinced nine other men to join him, and they played a five-on-five soccer game in April 1894.

There's a common saying about soccer in Brazil: "England invented it. The Brazilians perfected it." English soccer was formal and controlled, but as the Brazilians learned to play it, they developed a style that relied more on movement and individual skill. Brazil was the last country in the Western world to abolish slavery. It had only ended in 1888 and there was still a lot of racism in the country. Donohoe worked in a racially diverse factory and encouraged other workers at the factory to play. But all of the early formal soccer games in Brazil were reserved for

British players and members of the upper class. Still, other people and former slaves could see how much fun soccer was and began to play their own games. Then, in 1904, when an Athletic Club was formed in Bangu, the Bangu Atlético Clube became the first team in Brazil to select its players regardless of race.

Today in Brazil, the top soccer league is Campeonato Brasileiro Série A, but it's known more popularly as Brasileirão. Founded in 1959, it's made up of the top 20 teams in Brazil. The best teams in recent years have been Corinthians and São Paulo, but the best teams traditionally have been Santos FC and Palmeiras. All of these teams are based in São Paulo.

FIFA Rules the World

Soccer's first international games were played between teams from England and Scotland in 1870 and 1872. As the game spread around the

SÃO PAULO PLAYERS DEFEND AGAINST TOLUCA IN BRAZIL'S BRASILEIRÃO.

world, there was more and more interest in organizing games between teams from different countries. This was especially true in Europe, where the distances were not so great and it was relatively easy to visit other countries by train. There weren't any airplanes, and it could take a week or more to cross the ocean by ship.

By the start of the 20th century, many of the soccer associations in European countries were beginning to see the value of one large group to organize international matches and make sure that they were fair for everyone. On May 21, 1904, the Fédération Internationale de Football Association was created in Paris, France. The seven countries to start it all were Belgium, Denmark, France, the Netherlands (Holland), Spain, Sweden, and Switzerland. Today, with 211 different countries involved, the federation has more members than the United Nations! It's now based in Switzerland instead of France, but the French name is still used—although every-one knows it best as FIFA.

OPENING CEREMONIES OF THE FIFA CONGRESS IN MEXICO IN 2016

But the main reason that FIFA was formed was to organize international matches. FIFA runs all sorts of tournaments, for men, women, and children, all across the globe. Its biggest event, held every four years, is the World Cup.

SOCCER FOR SURVIVAL

BEFORE HE BECAME THE PRESIDENT OF SOUTH AFRICA, Nelson Mandela spent 27 years in prison. He was in jail because he was fighting for his rights and the rights of his people, who had very little freedom because of their race.

NELSON MANDELA

Mandela was sent to South Africa's notorious Robben Island prison in 1964. Soccer became a way for the prisoners to do something they loved, but it wasn't easy. Many prisoners were beaten or starved just for asking to be allowed to play. At first, they had to keep their games secret. They played quietly in their cells with balls made of paper, cardboard, and rags. When they were finally allowed to play outside, they organized teams and leagues that ran for years. The games gave the prisoners hope that life would get better. "Soccer is more than just a game," Mandela would later say. "The energy, passion, and dedication this game created made us feel alive and triumphant despite the situation we found ourselves in."

URUGUAY DEFEATED HOLLAND 2–1 IN SEMIFINAL ACTION.

SEMIFINAL ACTION FROM THE 1924 PARIS OLYMPICS

How the World Cup Started

Soccer's World Cup is the largest single-sport event on Earth. It's even bigger than the Super Bowl. Only the Olympics, with its many sports, attracts a bigger audience. More than three million fans have filled the stands at each of the last several World Cup games. For the 2014 World Cup in Brazil, a record-setting audience of just over one billion people watched at least some of the championship game on television or on a mobile device. In both 2010 and 2014, over 3.2 billion people tuned in on TV at some point during the tournament. The World Cup hasn't always attracted such huge audiences. In fact, it was even hard to get some of the top soccer countries to send their teams when the World Cup started in 1930! The first international soccer tournaments were held as part of the Olympics from 1900 to 1920. They weren't very successful. But at the 1924 Summer Olympics in Paris, a total of 22 different countries from all over the world took part in the Olympic soccer tournament. It marked the first time that countries from more than just Europe or North America had sent soccer teams to the Olympics. Big crowds turned out, with between 50,000 and 60,000 fans jamming the stadium for the final game to see Uruguay from South America defeat Switzerland from Europe 3–0 in the gold medal final. But even this tournament wasn't a total success. Olympic sports were only for amateur athletes in those days. Amateurs didn't accept money for playing sports, and anyone who was a professional was not allowed to play. England had won gold medals in 1908 and 1912 with a national amateur team, but chose not to send a team to Paris in 1924, since all the best

CONSTRUCTION OF A WORLD CUP STADIUM IN RUSSIA

HOME FIELD ADVANTAGE

MARK GEIGER

Similar to the Olympic Games, there are usually many countries that place a bid to host each World Cup. In a way, the bids that every country makes are like a presentation in your classroom at school. Each country has to show the committee that makes the decision why it should be the one allowed to host the event. In their bids, countries will describe the stadiums and facilities that will be used, and they will explain how their country will be able to handle the millions of people that will come to watch the World Cup live. The committee makes its decision for each World Cup many years in advance so the host country can get to work. It costs a lot of money and takes a lot of work to prepare for the World Cup. Stadiums and training facilities are built or improved for the teams and games. Roads, railways, and airports are upgraded to handle the traffic. Hotels are built to make sure everyone has a place to stay. It can cost billions of dollars!

In the end, countries believe that it's worth the money spent because of the huge amount of money that will be invested back into the country's economy once the event kicks off.

players in that country got paid to play soccer.

Still, the success of the 1924 Olympic soccer tournament was an inspiration to FIFA president Jules Rimet. Rimet had grown up in Paris and became president of FIFA in 1921. He was in favor of a world championship tournament that would feature all the best players whether they were paid a salary or not, but it took him many years to convince his fellow members. Finally, on May 26, 1928, FIFA approved the creation of the World Cup. The first one was held in July 1930.

Six different countries applied to host the inaugural World Cup. Five were in Europe: Italy, Hungary, the Netherlands (Holland), Spain, and Sweden. Uruguay also wanted to be the host country, and argued that it was the most deserving. Not only had it won the 1924 Olympic gold medal in soccer, it had won it again in 1928. On top of that, 1930 marked the 100th anniversary of Uruguay becoming an independent country. Celebrations were already being planned, and hosting the World Cup would be a great part of that. FIFA agreed and awarded the first World Cup to Uruguay. All the games would be played in the capital city of Montevideo. The world waited eagerly for the first World Cup, but there would be problems along the way. In October 1929, the U.S. stock market crashed and the world was plunged into the Great Depression.

EARLY OLYMPIC SOCCER

SOCCER WASN'T PART OF THE FIRST MODERN OLYMPICS in 1896, but a small tournament was held the first time the Olympics were in Paris in 1900. Only three teams were there, and just two games were played! Upton Park FC from England represented Great Britain and they

BRITAIN VERSUS DENMARK AT THE 1908 OLYMPICS

beat USFSA XI from France 4–0. Then USFS XI beat the University of Brussels, who represented Belgium, 6–4. No medals were awarded at the time, but today, England is credited with the gold medal, France has the silver, and Belgium has the bronze. In a way, the soccer tournament was even smaller when the Olympics were held in St. Louis, Missouri, U.S.A., in 1904. There were three teams again, but two of them were from St. Louis. The Galt Football Club from Canada beat Christian Brothers College 7–0 and St. Rose Parish 4–0 to win the gold medal. The 1908 London Olympics marked the first time that national soccer teams competed at the Olympics.

OLYMPIC SOCCER TODAY

THE 1984 SUMMER OLYMPICS IN LOS ANGELES marked the first time that professional athletes were allowed to compete. Since then, FIFA has wanted to make sure that the World Cup is still the best soccer tournament in the world. So compromises have had to be made at the Olympics. In the men's competition, countries have to field younger teams, with only three players allowed to be above the age of 23. The Summer Games in Atlanta, Georgia, U.S.A., in 1996 marked the first time that there was a women's Olympic tournament. American women won the gold medal in 1996, 2004, 2008 and 2012, with a silver medal in 2000. Canadian women won bronze medals at the last two Olympics in 2012 and 2016. There is no age limit on women's soccer teams at the Olympics.

AMERICAN WOMEN CELEBRATE GOLD AT THE 2012 SUMMER OLYMPICS.

CANADA VERSUS FRANCE FOR BRONZE AT THE 2012 SUMMER OLYMPICS

It was one of the worst economic times in history, and many countries that might have wanted to attend the first World Cup found that there were more important things to spend their money on than paying for long ocean voyages for their national soccer teams. In the end, only 12 other teams came to Uruguay, and six of them—Argentina, Bolivia, Brazil, Chile, Paraguay, and Peru—were from neighboring countries in South America. Only four teams traveled to Uruguay from Europe: Belgium, France, Romania, and Yugoslavia. In North America, the United States and Mexico sent a team. Canada didn't.

Uruguay versus Argentina was the final that everyone in those two countries had been hoping for. Not only were they neighbors in South America, but they were big rivals. Argentina was looking for revenge after losing the gold-medal game to Uruguay at the 1928 Olympics. Ten special boats had been set aside to take fans from Argentina to Uruguay for the final game, but they weren't nearly enough. Somewhere between 10,000 and 15,000 fans made the trip, and the harbor in Montevideo was so jammed that not every boat had even reached land by the time the game started around 2:15 on the afternoon of July 30. The gates of the stadium had opened six hours early at a little after 8 a.m., and the stadium was full by noon. Official attendance was 93,000.

How heated was the rivalry between Uruguay and Argentina? The two teams couldn't even decide on whose soccer ball they should use! The referee finally had to declare that each half would be played with a different ball. He then tossed a coin to determine that it would be the ball from Argentina in the first half and Uruguay's ball in the second. Turns out the ball may have been pretty important, as Argentina

USA! USA! USA!

WITH HIS THREE GOALS against Paraguay on July 17, 1930, Bert Patenaude became the first player in World Cup history to score a hat trick. However, it took nearly 76 years for the American star to be recognized for his feat! That's because of a discrepancy in how the second American goal was credited in the 3–0 win over Paraguay. The United States Soccer Federation always credited the goal to Patenaude, but FIFA had given it to his teammate Tom Florie. Other records say a player from Paraguay had scored in his own net. Patenaude always believed he had scored it, and as his son once said: "He wasn't the type of man who would've taken credit for something that he didn't do." Patenaude died on November 4, 1974 ,without ever getting official credit. Eventually, on November 10, 2006, FIFA announced that, after lengthy research, it had changed its ruling. Patenaude finally had his hat trick!

THE 1930 USA WORLD CUP TEAM

BERT PATENAUDE

IT TOOK **NEARLY 76 YEARS** FOR THE AMERICAN STAR TO BE RECOGNIZED FOR HIS FEAT!

THE FIFA WORLD CUP TROPHY IS MADE OF 18-KARAT GOLD

SPAIN CELEBRATES WINNING THE WORLD CUP IN 2010.

held a 2–1 lead at halftime but Uruguay rallied in the second half for a 4–2 victory.

How the World Cup Works Today

Today the World Cup is a month-long tournament held every four years, usually in June or July. FIFA now has 211 member nations, but only 32 countries are represented at the World Cup. (It will expand to 48 countries in 2026.) So who decides which countries get to go?

Ever since the first World Cup, the host country has been guaranteed a spot in the

EAST TIMOR IN QUALIFY-ING ACTION FOR THE 2018 WORLD CUP

tournament. It used to be that the defending champions were given a free pass, too. That was changed in 2006. Now, all 31 countries except the host country have to earn their way to the World Cup through a series of qualifying matches. Qualification tournaments are played all around the world, in six different geographic zones. These tournaments are held over a two-year span, and usually begin one year after the last World Cup ended and three years before the next one starts. For the 2018 World Cup in Russia, a total of 208 countries took part in more than 800 qualification matches.

After the final field of 32 national teams is determined, the World Cup begins with the group stage. The teams are split into eight different groups of four teams each. FIFA uses a system of points to rank all of its national teams, and these rankings help spread out the world's top teams into the different groups. The rest of the teams are assigned to groups at random, although some rules are applied based on geography to try to keep things even.

Once the groups have been set up, the World Cup begins with a round-robin schedule. This means that every team plays one game against each of the other three teams in its group. Since 1994, teams receive three points for every game they win, one point for every tie (usually called a draw in soccer), and no points for a loss. When every team has completed their three games, the two teams with the most points in each group move on. The bottom two teams are eliminated. If any teams are tied in their group standings, the ties are broken based on the number of goals scored and given up.

The second round of the World Cup is often called the Round of 16 because 16 teams have advanced this far. In this round, the first-place teams from the group round play against a second-place team from a different group. This begins the knockout portion of the World Cup, where every team needs a win to stay alive. If they lose, they get knocked out. The eight winning teams move on to the quarterfinals, and the four teams that win there advance to the semifinals. After that, the two teams that lose the semifinals play against each other in the third-place match. The two teams that win the semifinals move on to the final and play for the World Cup championship.

A+ REF

MARK GEIGER

THE REFEREES GO THROUGH A SIMILAR PROCESS as the teams to get appointed to the World Cup. Approximately two years before the next World Cup, 50 or 60 referees and their assistant referees from around the world are selected to be in the World Cup project. These referees come together to attend seminars. It's like going to school. The referees all review how the Laws of the Game should be interpreted and applied. The goal is to have all the referees thinking the same way so that there will be uniformity and consistency at the World Cup. In these seminars, the referees are marked and graded in practice sessions on the field where teams of players simulate game situations. Finally, the referees take video tests on fouls and offsides and take written tests to check their knowledge of the Laws of the Game. In addition to the seminars, the referees are evaluated in all their matches in their country and confederation, and each referee participates in a FIFA tournament the year before the World Cup. All these events together help determine who are the best referees in the world and who should be selected for the World Cup.

A FIFA TRAINING SESSION FOR REFEREES AND ASSISTANT REFEREES

SOCCER'S SIX ZONES

ARCTIC

EU

NORTH
AMERICA

ATLANTIC
OCEAN

AF

PACIFIC
OCEAN

SOUTH
AMERICA

Asian Football Confederation (AFC)

Confederación Sudamericana de Fútbol (CONMEBOL)

Confédération Africaine de Football (CAF)

Oceania Football Confederation (OFC)

The Confederation of North, Central American
and Caribbean Association Football (CONCACAF)

Union des Associations Européennes de Football (UEFA)

Not in a zone

OCEAN

ROPE

ASIA

RICA

PACIFIC
OCEAN

INDIAN
OCEAN

AUSTRALIA

FIFA has divided the world map into six different zones, or confederations, for soccer. Based mainly on the world's continents, each confederation stages its own competitions at the club and international levels. In addition, special tournaments are held within each confederation that determine which countries qualify for the World Cup.

GET IN THE GAME

WHILE SOCCER WAS SPREADING AROUND THE WORLD from the 1860s to the 1890s, baseball was becoming known as America's National Pastime. At the same time in Canada, hockey was developing into its national game. The first soccer league in the world was organized in England in 1885, but let's explore when similar things were going on in baseball and hockey. Can you match up the year on the right with the description on the left?

1. The first American baseball league was formed. (It was known as the National Association)

2. The National League was formed.

3. The American League was formed.

4. The World Series began.

5. The first professional baseball team was formed (the Cincinnati Red Stockings).

6. The first Canadian hockey league was formed. (It was known as the Amateur Hockey Association.)

7. The Stanley Cup was awarded for the first time.

8. The National Hockey League was formed.

a: 1869

e: 1893

b: 1871

f: 1901

c: 1876

g: 1903

d: 1886

h: 1917

ANSWERS: 1. b; 2. c; 3. f; 4. g; 5. a; 6. d; 7. e; 8. h.

THE OFFICIAL ATTENDANCE FOR THE
FIRST WORLD CUP CHAMPIONSHIP GAME
IN 1930 WAS 93,000 PEOPLE.
LET'S SEE HOW THAT COMPARES
TO EARLY CHAMPIONSHIPS IN THE UNITED STATES.

FIRST WORLD SERIES (1903)
100,429
for eight games

(average 12,554 per game)

FIRST NFL CHAMPIONSHIP GAME (1933)
26,000

FIRST SUPER BOWL (1967)
61,946

THE HIGHEST ATTENDANCE EVER FOR A WORLD CUP GAME IS 173,850

for the final game between Brazil and Uruguay in Maracanã Stadium in Rio de Janeiro, on July 16, 1950. Let's see how that compares to other championships in the United States.

Indianapolis 500. Official attendance not announced. (Indianapolis Motor Speedway holds over 250,000 people.)

Kentucky Derby 2015, Churchill Downs: 170,513.

Super Bowl XIV (1980) Pittsburgh vs. Dallas, Rose Bowl Stadium: 103,985.

World Series 1959 Game Five Los Angeles Dodgers vs. Chicago White Sox, Los Angeles Coliseum: 92,706.

A HUGE CROWD ATTENDED THE 1950 WORLD CUP FINAL.

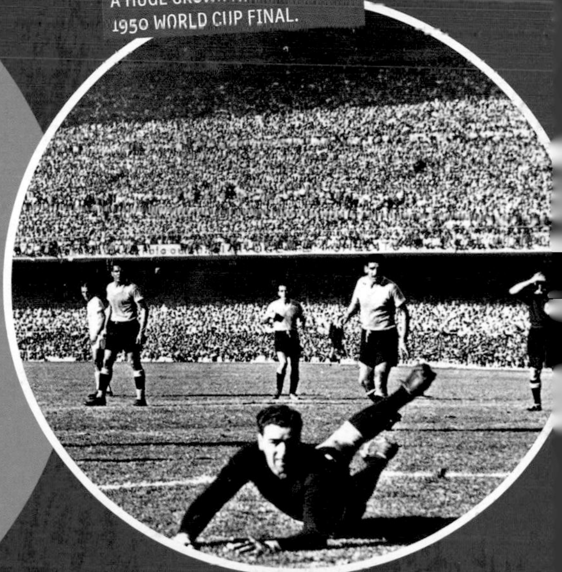

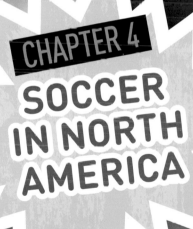

CHAPTER 4

SOCCER IN NORTH AMERICA

JULIE JOHNSTON (#8, NOW JULIE ERTZ) OF THE UNITED STATES BATTLES FOR THE BALL WITH NICHELLE PRINCE OF CANADA DURING THE CHAMPIONSHIP FINAL OF THE 2016 CONCACAF WOMEN'S OLYMPIC QUALIFYING MATCH.

INTRODUCTION

ALTHOUGH SOCCER IS THE WORLD'S GAME,

its popularity in North America has often been overshadowed by other sports. American football, baseball, basketball, and hockey have usually dominated ticket sales, merchandise sales, and television ratings. Recently, though, this has begun to change.

MARK GEIGER

There have been times in the past when soccer has been popular with American sports fans. From 1968 to 1984, there was a professional soccer league known as the North American Soccer League (NASL). International superstars such as Brazilian legend Pelé and German great Franz Beckenbauer graced the soccer fields of the United States and Canada during this time, but the league didn't last. When the NASL shut down in 1984, soccer's popularity in the United States declined again, but it began to re-emerge and grow during the 1994 FIFA World Cup.

The general American public was re-introduced to soccer in a big way when the United States hosted the World Cup that year. Fans from around the world paraded through the streets of American cities. Teams brought with them their passion for the sport, their love of their teams and players, and their pride in their countries and national colors. This—along with the growing success of the United States national team—ignited a flame in the hearts of Americans for soccer. With this momentum and spirit, Major League Soccer (MLS) was born in 1996.

In its early years, Major League Soccer was very small compared to the other sports that dominated North America. There were only 10 teams spread out throughout the United States. Many of the teams played in large stadiums they shared with NFL football teams. Today, most MLS clubs have their own more intimate stadiums built specifically for soccer. These stadiums don't hold as many fans, but they put everyone so much closer to the action on the field. This has helped the league to grow, creating more fans, with more teams in new cities, and building greater rivalries.

Players are making more money, which allows the best American and Canadian stars to play at home. These better salaries have also helped to attract international players in their prime. Attendance numbers and television ratings grow every year, and MLS games are watched live in approximately 170 countries.

Yes, soccer has truly arrived in North America. Its popularity continues to grow, and it will be great to see where the sport is in another 20 years. Maybe it will be competing to be the number one sport in North America, as it is in the rest of the world.

IN ITS EARLY YEARS, **MAJOR LEAGUE SOCCER** WAS VERY SMALL COMPARED TO THE OTHER SPORTS THAT DOMINATED NORTH AMERICA.

DAVID VILLA OF NEW YORK CITY FC SHOOTS FOR A GOAL.

COULD THE SUPER BOWL EXIST WITHOUT THE NATIONAL FOOTBALL LEAGUE?

Or the World Series without Major League Baseball? It's hard to imagine. Why would there be a big championship if there was no league playing the sport?

The World Cup is so much bigger than any one league, but not having a league was an issue when FIFA awarded the 1994 World Cup to the United States. Americans would get to host the world's biggest soccer championship, but there was no major professional league in the United States at the time. FIFA made it a condition of hosting the World Cup that

the U.S. Soccer Federation (which is simply known as U.S. Soccer and oversees all levels of soccer in the United States) had to establish a new league. That's how Major League Soccer was born.

The MLS Story

Major League Soccer—known as MLS for short—is the highest level of men's professional soccer in the United States and Canada. MLS began in 1996 with 10 teams but doubled in size to 20 teams by 2015, with 17 in the United States and three in Canada. Two more American teams were added in 2017, with another coming on board in 2018. A 24th team is planned by 2020.

The MLS season stretches from March to October. Each team plays 34 games. Playoffs are held in November and into December, ending with the championship known as the MLS

FAN #1

THE SAN JOSE CLASH BATTLE DC UNITED IN THE INAUGURAL MLS GAME.

WorldCupUSA94

CROWDS FILL ROSE BOWL STADIUM DURING THE 1994 WORLD CUP FINAL.

Cup. There's also an All-Star Game held every summer. Since 2005, the format for the MLS All-Star Game has been for a team picked from the league's best players to play against one of the top club teams from a league in Europe.

MLS kicked off its first season on April 6, 1996. There were only 10 teams in the league, but some names were familiar to American soccer fans. The teams were made up of many American heroes from the 1994 World Cup team. Players such as Marcelo Balboa, John Harkes, Cobi Jones, Alexi Lalas, Tony Meola, Joe-Max Moore, Tab Ramos, and Eric Wynalda, and others from the 1994 U.S. roster, were spread throughout this new league. Several of these players remained in the league for many years to come. The first MLS game saw the San Jose Clash (now known as the San Jose Earthquakes) beat Washington's D.C. United 1–0. The first goal in MLS history was scored by Eric Wynalda.

TONY MEOLA

TONY MEOLA

GOALKEEPER TONY MEOLA is one of the best American soccer players of all time. He was a member of the U.S. national team for 18 years from 1988 to 2006 and played in exactly 100 games. Meola played at the World Cup in 1990, 1994, and 2002. He began his MLS career the league's first season of 1996. Meola played for the New York MetroStars (now the New York Red Bulls) and led the league with nine shutouts that season. His best season came in 2000 as a member of the Kansas City Wizards (now Sporting Kansas City). Meola set an MLS record with 16 shutouts that year. He not only led Kansas City to the MLS Cup championship, but he was named the league's best goalkeeper, its most valuable player, and the MVP of the MLS Cup. Meola played in MLS for 11 seasons.

MEOLA WAS NAMED THE LEAGUE'S **BEST GOALKEEPER**, ITS **MOST VALUABLE PLAYER**, AND THE **MVP OF THE MLS CUP.**

ERIC WYNALDA

MARK GEIGER

A TEAM BY ANY OTHER NAME

MANY OF THE ORIGINAL MLS TEAMS have changed their names over the years. For example, the Columbus Crew has become Columbus Crew SC; the Dallas Burn have become FC Dallas; the Kansas City Wizards have become Sporting KC; the NY/NJ MetroStars have become the New York Red Bulls; the San Jose Clash have become the San Jose Earthquakes. There are many reasons for the name changes. Sometimes the team is looking for a new identity or to keep up with the times and be more modern. In many cases, the new names are more in keeping with soccer teams from all around the world. Sometimes these name changes come with changes in team colors and logos, too. These rebrands often help energize the fans and introduce more enthusiasm for the teams. Which team will be the next to re-create itself as the league continues to grow and expand?

The first MLS season of 1996 also featured several international stars from the 1994 World Cup. Players such as Jorge Campos, Mauricio Cienfuegos, Marco Etcheverry, Eduardo Hurtado, and Carlos Valderrama helped bring international attention to MLS. Jorge Campos was a particular favorite. He was a goalkeeper from Mexico who joined the Los Angeles Galaxy. Campos was known for his brightly colored outfits and his acrobatic style. He was only about 5-foot-6, but his athleticism, his speed, and his leaping ability enabled him to block shots that seemed impossible to reach. Campos hasn't played soccer since 2004, but he has remained so popular that he's continued to appear as a player in FIFA video games.

Carlos Valderrama was a veteran player from Colombia who'd been playing professional soccer since 1981. He was instantly recognizable to American fans because

CARLOS VALDERRAMA

of his long, crazy, frizzy blonde hair—but he was a great player, too. Valderrama was named the most valuable player of the first MLS season in 1996 and remained in the league until 2002.

Slowly but surely, MLS began to make a name for itself alongside the NFL, the NBA, the NHL, and Major League Baseball. The 1994 World Cup was the reason MLS got started, but it was the strong showing of the American team at the 2002 World Cup in South Korea that really helped the league take off.

The United States began the 2002 tournament with a 3–2 upset win over Portugal, who had been a favorite to win the World Cup that year. Next came a 1–1 tie with South Korea in front of nearly 61,000 fans of the host country. Even though the Americans lost their final Group Round game, they still advanced to the tournament's Round of 16. There, they faced their CONCACAF rivals from Mexico. It was the first time that the two countries had ever met in a World Cup game, and the Americans beat Mexico 2–0.

ALEXI LALAS

LOS ANGELES GALAXY VERSUS NEW ENGLAND REVOLUTION IN THE 2002 MLS CUP

MINI CUP MARK GEIGER

TODAY, IT'S NOT UNHEARD OF TO SEE CROWDS of more than 50,000 fans at an MLS game. It's not an everyday occurrence, but there are some matchups that draw big crowds. The Cascadia Cup is the trophy from a mini tournament held within the MLS season between the Portland Timbers, Seattle Sounders, and Vancouver Whitecaps. The Cascadia Cup was actually introduced in 2004, before any of these teams were even in MLS. (The rivalry dates all the way back to the days of the original North American Soccer League!) For these matches today, the stadiums are opened up to allow more fans to come and watch. Busloads of spectators from the visiting team's city converge on the host city. The environment for the spectators, players, coaches, and referees is intense and exciting. These games are played with a little more energy and bite and give the fans in the stands a truly wonderful experience.

MLS TEAMS

Vancouver Whitecaps FC, BRITISH COLUMBIA

Seattle Sounders FC, WASHINGTON

Portland Timbers, OREGON

Real Salt Lake, UTAH

Colorado Rapids, COLORADO

San Jose Earthquakes, CALIFORNIA

Los Angeles FC, CALIFORNIA

LA Galaxy, CALIFORNIA

FC Dallas, TEXAS

CANADA

UNITED

MEXICO

MLS CONFERENCE
- Eastern
- Western

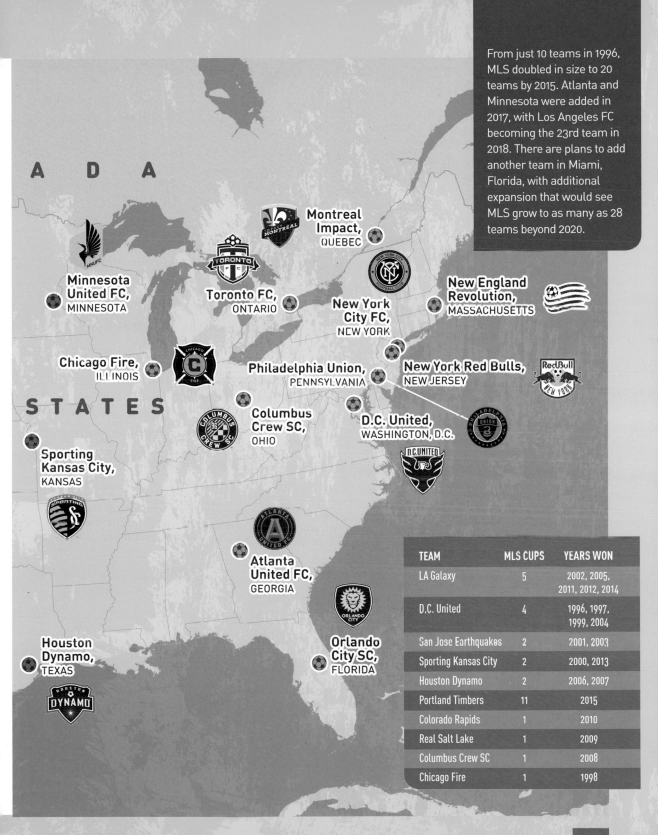

From just 10 teams in 1996, MLS doubled in size to 20 teams by 2015. Atlanta and Minnesota were added in 2017, with Los Angeles FC becoming the 23rd team in 2018. There are plans to add another team in Miami, Florida, with additional expansion that would see MLS grow to as many as 28 teams beyond 2020.

A D A

Montreal Impact, QUEBEC

Minnesota United FC, MINNESOTA

Toronto FC, ONTARIO

New York City FC, NEW YORK

New England Revolution, MASSACHUSETTS

Chicago Fire, ILLINOIS

Philadelphia Union, PENNSYLVANIA

New York Red Bulls, NEW JERSEY

S T A T E S

Columbus Crew SC, OHIO

D.C. United, WASHINGTON, D.C.

Sporting Kansas City, KANSAS

Atlanta United FC, GEORGIA

Orlando City SC, FLORIDA

Houston Dynamo, TEXAS

TEAM	MLS CUPS	YEARS WON
LA Galaxy	5	2002, 2005, 2011, 2012, 2014
D.C. United	4	1996, 1997, 1999, 2004
San Jose Earthquakes	2	2001, 2003
Sporting Kansas City	2	2000, 2013
Houston Dynamo	2	2006, 2007
Portland Timbers	11	2015
Colorado Rapids	1	2010
Real Salt Lake	1	2009
Columbus Crew SC	1	2008
Chicago Fire	1	1998

LANDON DONOVAN

DURING HIS CAREER, LANDON DONOVAN scored more goals than any other American player in international soccer games. Donovan was taught how to play by his brother Josh as a young boy. He joined his first team when he was just five years old and scored seven goals in his very first game! His first international tournament was the 1999 FIFA U-17 World Cup and he won the Ballon d'Or (gold ball) as the best player. In his World Cup debut in 2002, Donovan received the award as the tournament's best young player. Donovan began his pro career in Germany in 1999 but came home to play for MLS in 2001. He starred with the LA Galaxy from 2005 to 2014, winning the MLS Cup in 2005, 2011, 2012, 2014. (He also won it with San Jose in 2001 and 2003.) Donovan retired after the 2014 season but returned to the Galaxy in 2016.

LANDON DONOVAN

LANDON JOINED HIS FIRST TEAM WHEN HE WAS JUST **FIVE YEARS OLD** AND SCORED SEVEN GOALS IN HIS VERY FIRST GAME.

MLS stars Brian McBride and Landon Donovan scored the goals. The win over Mexico marked the first time that the United States won a knockout game at the World Cup! It was also the first American shutout since a legendary 1–0 win over England in 1950.

With the win, the U.S. advanced to the quarterfinals, and even though it lost that game 1–0 to Germany, it was the best American performance at the World Cup since it had reached the semifinals at the first tournament in 1930. Unlike in those early years, American fans were definitely paying attention this time. Big crowds started showing up at MLS games, and when the LA Galaxy beat the New England Revolution for the championship in the MLS Cup that year, a record crowd of more than 61,000 fans were there for the game.

The next big boost for MLS came in 2007. There were actually two big boosts that year, and this time, they came from outside the United States. One was that, after 11 years, MLS decided it was time to grow beyond the U.S. border and truly become a North American league. The Toronto Football Club joined MLS in 2007. It is usually known as Toronto FC, or sometimes just TFC for short. Sometimes people call the team the Reds for its bright red home colors. Its fans often dress in red too, filling Toronto's BMO Field for every game. Toronto FC was the lowest ranking team in MLS in its first season, but the fans never stopped supporting the team. Today it's one of the best teams in the league.

The second big addition to MLS in 2007 gave the league an even bigger boost. It came when

ARMANDO COOPER OF TORONTO FC VERSUS SEATTLE SOUNDERS IN THE 2016 MLS CUP

OTHER COMPETITIONS MARK GEIGER

SOCCER LEAGUES ALL AROUND THE WORLD have time built into their regular schedules to allow their teams to play in other competitions too. MLS is no different, with its teams eligible to play in the Confederation of North, Central American and Caribbean Association Football (CONCACAF) Champions League each year against teams from Mexico, the Caribbean, and Central America. The United States can send four teams to the CONCACAF series. Three teams earn their spots based on the MLS standings and playoffs. A fourth American team is determined through a competition known as the U.S. Open Cup, which includes teams from MLS, North American Soccer League (NASL), and United Soccer League (USL). The MLS teams in Canada—Toronto FC, Montreal Impact, and Vancouver Whitecaps—play a Canadian Championship series with the Ottawa Fury and FC Edmonton of the NASL to determine one Canadian team for the CONCACAF series.

NEW YORK COSMOS PLAYER RAÚL GONZÁLEZ BLANCO MOVES TOWARD THE GOAL IN A U.S. OPEN CUP MATCH AGAINST THE NEW YORK RED BULLS, JULY 2015.

OTHER NORTH AMERICAN LEAGUES

MARK GEIGER

JUST LIKE THE NATIONAL HOCKEY LEAGUE and Major League Baseball have minor league systems, there are minor soccer leagues in North America too. The North American Soccer League (NASL) is considered a Division II league under Major League Soccer. The NASL currently has teams in the United States, Canada, and Puerto Rico. It has no direct relationship to MLS. The United Soccer League (USL) is a Division II league, also beneath MLS. It has 30 teams across the United States and Canada. All its teams are either owned by or partnered with an MLS team. The two leagues can loan players back and forth to give younger players a better chance to develop.

THE NEW YORK RED BULLS (MLS) BATTLE THE NEW YORK COSMOS (NASL) IN A U.S. OPEN CUP GAME.

the LA Galaxy lured one of the greatest international players in soccer away from the top leagues in Europe.

David Beckham and MLS

England's David Beckham may not have been the best player in soccer when he joined the LA Galaxy in 2007, but he was still a very good one. And he was definitely the most famous. Even people who didn't know anything about soccer knew David Beckham. His wife, Victoria, was famous, too. She'd been a member of a music group called the Spice Girls. The two were always pictured on magazine covers. They designed their own clothing brands and had their own line of fragrances. Beckham appeared in commercials for soft drinks, sports shoes, fast-food restaurants, and fancy fashions. He and Victoria also did a lot of work for worldwide charities.

Beckham began playing professional soccer when he was 17 years old and joined Manchester United in 1992. Between 1992 and 2003, Beckham led Man U to six Premier League championships. In 2003, Beckham signed with Real Madrid in Spain's La Liga. He played there for four years, winning a championship with them during his last season of 2006–07. Beckham also played for England's national team from 1996 to 2009. He played 115 matches, and he was captain of the team for 59 of them. He played at the World Cup in 1998, 2002, and 2006 and is the only player in English history to score a goal in three different World Cup tournaments.

On the pitch, Beckham had a few moves he could make better than anyone else in soccer. He was known for his great crosses, making long passes from near the sidelines toward the front of his opponent's goal. He was also known for scoring on free kicks by putting so much spin

BECKHAM BEGAN PLAYING PROFESSIONAL SOCCER WHEN HE WAS 17 YEARS OLD.

DAVID BECKHAM

DAVID BECKHAM WITH THE BALL
DURING HIS FIRST MLS GAME

THE BECKHAM EFFECT

MARK GEIGER

DAVID BECKHAM BROUGHT A HUGE NEW GROUP OF FANS to Major League Soccer. People showed up by the thousands to see him. Attendance numbers soared to incredible heights. Beckham made his MLS debut on August 9, 2007, at RFK Stadium in Washington, D.C. I happened to be the fourth official for this game and the stadium was electric. There were more than 46,000 people there to watch. It was a sellout crowd and more than three times D.C. United's usual attendance at the time. Beckham started on the bench, but every move he made was closely watched. There was a camera on him at all times, and when he got up to start warming up, the video was projected on the big screen in the stadium. The noise from the crowd was so loud, you would have thought he just scored the winning goal at the World Cup! This enthusiasm and energy followed David Beckham from stadium to stadium. His presence in MLS kick-started a wave of high-profile international players.

on the ball that it would curl around the line of players blocking its path to the goal. This is known as bending the ball, and he was so famous for doing it that a movie in 2002 was called *Bend It Like Beckham*.

To bring Beckham to North America, MLS had to pass a new rule. In order to keep its costs under control, MLS has a salary cap. In 2007, the cap meant that no team could spend more than $2.7 million in salaries— for its entire roster. (A new agreement reached in 2015 allows the salary cap to grow to $4.24 million per team by 2019). But the league knew that the best soccer stars in the world could make a lot more money than that all by themselves playing for teams in Europe. So, MLS passed the Designated Player Rule. People often refer to it as the Beckham Rule. The rule allows MLS teams to designate certain players they can sign to big contracts that go well beyond the salary cap— as long as there are no more than three of them on the team.

The contract that David Beckham signed in 2007 gave him a guaranteed salary of $6.5 million a year for five years. That's a total of $32.5 million. Was it worth it? Well, when Beckham came to Los Angeles to play for the Galaxy, he brought a record level of interest to MLS. Even though he missed a lot of games due to an injury that first season, Beckham drew giant crowds to all the Galaxy games even if he was just sitting on the bench.

Beckham continued to play in Europe at other times of the year, but he returned to Los Angeles to play for the Galaxy every season from 2008 to 2012. Together with Landon Donovan, he helped the Galaxy win the MLS Cup in 2011. They won it again in 2012 in Beckham's final game with the team. He played one last season in France in 2013 with Paris Saint-Germain and won another championship there in his very last game.

In all, David Beckham won 10 league championships with four

SOCCER SUPERSTARS

DAVID BECKHAM was one of the first high-profile players to play in MLS, but he was not the last. Since his signing, many more world-class soccer players have come to the U.S.A. and Canada. Each one has contributed to the popularity and growth of Major League Soccer in a variety of ways, both on and off the field. The list of players includes such names as Cuauhtémoc Blanco, Giovani dos Santos, Didier Drogba, Steven Gerrard, Sebastian Giovinco, Thierry Henry, Kaká, Robbie Keane, Frank Lampard, Andrea Pirlo, and David Villa. These Designated Players have not only drawn larger crowds to MLS games and made world-class moves on the field, but they've also raised the skill level of the entire league. Younger players on each team get the opportunity to play every day in practice with these stars. They benefit from their leadership and guidance, and they improve as players by working with them day in and day out. Having these Designated Players has raised the overall level of play within Major League Soccer. It's also exciting to see who the next big signing will be!

DIDIER DROGBA

GIOVANI DOS SANTOS

different teams in four different countries during his 20-year professional career. His time in Los Angeles did a lot to increase soccer's profile in the United States. You may not even know it, but it could be a big part of the reason that you're a soccer fan today. Even if Beckham didn't inspire you directly, he may have inspired your mom or dad, or your favorite player on your favorite team.

Early American Soccer Leagues

Even though there was no major soccer league in the country when the United States hosted the 1994 World Cup, there had been American soccer leagues long before then. How long before? Twenty years? Thirty? Keep guessing. You have to go back a pretty long way!

The very first professional soccer league in the United States began 100 years before the 1994 World Cup in 1894. It was organized by six owners of National League baseball teams who wanted to keep their stadiums full after the baseball season ended.

They called their soccer league the American League of Professional Football. (There was no American League in baseball yet, and no National Football League either.) Even back then, the league's most popular team was bringing in players from Sheffield and Manchester in England. Unfortunately, this soccer league didn't work out. It only lasted for one season.

The first successful professional soccer league in the United States was the American Soccer League (ASL). Other leagues have used that same name over the years, but this one was the first. It operated from 1921 to 1933, but it didn't stretch across the entire United States like MLS does. All of its teams were based in or near New York City, New Jersey, Boston, and Philadelphia. Still, the ASL was a pretty big success for a while. Baseball was the favorite American sport back then, and college football was pretty popular, too. Pro football was still in its early days, with the

U.S.A. VERSUS BELGIUM AT THE 1930 WORLD CUP

U.S.A. VERSUS ARGENTINA IN THE 1930 WORLD CUP SEMIFINALS

NFL only starting up in 1920. In those days, the ASL was a big challenge to the NFL's popularity.

The American Soccer League featured many rich owners who were happy to spend their money bringing over star players from England and Scotland. And there was plenty of American talent, too. In fact, most of the players on the American team that did so well at the first World Cup in 1930, including Bert Patenaude, played for teams in the ASL. Unfortunately, battles with FIFA and U.S. Soccer—often over the salaries the ASL paid to lure players away from Europe—hurt the league. These so-called "Soccer Wars" angered many American soccer fans. They didn't like that U.S. Soccer sided with FIFA against the ASL in the salary battle. American fans soon turned away from soccer. Football became a lot more popular, and it would be a long time before soccer finally made a comeback.

PELÉ

One league that had success for a while was the North American Soccer League (NASL). It operated from 1968 to 1984. (The current league called the North American Soccer League began play in 2011 but has no connection to this original league.) Like MLS, the NASL had teams in the United States and Canada. The league was slowly beginning to grow in the early 1970s when it decided to make a bold move. The great Brazilian star Pelé had announced his retirement in 1974, but on June 10, 1975, he signed to play with the New York Cosmos in the NASL. Pelé was given a three-year contract worth $2.8 million. That's not a lot of money for a sports star today, but at the time it made Pelé the highest paid athlete in the world!

When Pelé played his first game for the Cosmos five days later, 10 million people watched on TV. It was the biggest audience ever for an American soccer game. Attendance all

ON JUNE 10, 1975, PELÉ SIGNED TO PLAY WITH THE NEW YORK COSMOS IN THE NASL.

PELÉ

A STAMP FROM AFRICA FEATURING PELÉ

around the league doubled during Pelé's three years with New York, and the Cosmos capped off his time with the team by winning the league championship in his final season of 1977.

After Pelé arrived in New York, other aging international soccer stars signed with NASL teams, too. They included Germany's Franz Beckenbauer and Gerd Müller; Johan Cruyff from the Netherlands (Holland); and George Best from England, to name just a few. But soon there were too many teams in the league paying too much money to too many players ... and they weren't drawing big enough crowds to pay for it. It was an important lesson. Today, even with the Designated Player Rule, the MSL salary cap ensures that the league doesn't suffer from the same problems as the NASL.

Although the original North American Soccer League hasn't existed since 1984, many of its team names still live on. The Portland Timbers, San Jose Earthquakes, Seattle Sounders, and Vancouver Whitecaps in MLS all have the same names as the teams in those cities from the NASL. Other team names from the old league (New York Cosmos, Tampa Bay Rowdies, and Fort Lauderdale Strikers) have reappeared in the new NASL.

AMERICAN MLS STARS

Before David Beckham arrived in Los Angeles, Major League Soccer had always marketed itself on the strength of its American stars. But as the league got stronger, and the United States started doing better in international events, the top leagues in Europe started luring away the best MLS players. So, the Designated Player Rule isn't just a way to bring top international stars to the United States, it's become a way to bring American stars back home!

JOZY ALTIDORE was born in Livingston, New Jersey, but grew up in Boca Raton, Florida, where he began playing soccer as a young boy. He has represented the United States at many international tournaments, including FIFA's U-17 and U-20 World Cup events, the 2008 Beijing Olympics, and the World Cup in 2010 and 2014. He began his MLS career with the New York Red Bulls in 2006 when he was still just 16 years old. Altidore quickly became a fan favorite in New York, but early in the 2008 season the Red Bulls

JOZY ALTIDORE

CLINT DEMPSEY

CLINT DEMPSEY grew up in Nacogdoches, Texas, and played soccer on dirt fields with the large local Hispanic community there. As a teenager, he played in a men's league in Mexico. His sister Jennifer was a top youth tennis player who died of a brain disorder when she was only 16. Dempsey used this tragedy as motivation to become as good as he could at soccer to honor her memory. He's become one of the best players in U.S. soccer history!

Dempsey made his first appearance with the U.S. men's senior national team in November 2004. He played at the World Cup in 2006, 2010, and 2014, and he was captain of the U.S. team in 2014.

Dempsey also began his MLS career in 2004. He was the league's rookie of the year that season while playing for the New England Revolution. He helped New England reach the MLS Cup in 2005 and 2006, but it lost the title each year. At the end of the 2006 season, the English club Fulham offered MLS a $4 million transfer fee. At the time, it was the most money ever paid for an MLS player. Dempsey spent seven seasons in England but returned to MLS in 2013 when the Seattle Sounders FC signed him to a four-year contract as a Designated Player.

agreed to let him join the Spanish team Villarreal of La Liga. The transfer fee for him was nearly $10 million! On November 1, 2008, Altidore became the first American player ever to score a goal in Spain's top soccer league.

Over the next few years, Altidore played for teams in Spain, Turkey, England, and Holland. He returned to MLS in 2015 when he joined Toronto FC as a Designated Player. Altidore scored two goals in his very first game with Toronto. He's continued to be one of the team's top scorers and helped Toronto become one of the league's top teams.

After playing eight years in Europe, **MICHAEL BRADLEY** joined Toronto FC as a Designated Player in 2014. He quickly became a team leader. It was Bradley who helped convince Jozy Altidore to come to Toronto. The two players had been teammates for a long time in the U.S. national soccer program.

Bradley was born in Princeton, New Jersey, where his father was the soccer coach at Princeton University. Bob Bradley would go on to coach teams in MLS and was the coach of the U.S. men's soccer team from late in 2006 to 2011. He has also coached teams in Europe and became the first American to coach a team in England's Premier League when he was hired as manager of Swansea City in 2016.

Michael Bradley established himself as a top U.S. player while his father was coach of the national team. He played in many key international matches beginning in 2007 and leading up to the World Cup in 2010. Even after his father was replaced as coach in 2011, Bradley continued to star for the U.S. team. He played at the World Cup again in 2014 and became captain of the American team in 2015.

MICHAEL BRADLEY

Women's Soccer History

We know that women have been playing soccer-like games since ancient times. It's believed that women also took part in medieval football games, too. Sadly, it hasn't always been easy for women to get the recognition they deserve in sports.

Some of the earliest stories of modern women's soccer date back to 1881 when games were played between teams from Scotland and England. Men found it strange to see women playing soccer in long skirts and bonnets—and they weren't very nice about it. Newspaper stories mocked the women's clothes and their style of play. Clearly these reporters believed that soccer was too rough a game for delicate ladies to play.

Opinions about what were suitable activities for women began to change during World War I, which lasted from 1914 to 1918. With so many men away fighting as soldiers, women were needed to work in factories. If they could do that, why couldn't they play soccer, too? Suddenly, women's games became quite popular. On the day after Christmas in 1920, a game between two women's teams in the English city of Liverpool drew a crowd of 53,000 fans. But instead of being good news for women's soccer, it turned out to be a disaster.

Were the men in charge of soccer in Britain jealous of the women's success? Were they worried that soccer would no longer be seen as a manly sport if women were playing it? Maybe. There were even some prominent British

ENGLAND'S PRESTON LADIES FOOTBALL CLUB IN 1939

BRENDA SEMPARE OF ENGLAND IN 1983

women who thought it was unladylike, and even unhealthy, for women to play soccer. Whatever the reasons, on December 5, 1921, the Football Association issued this ruling:

"Complaints have been made as to football being played by women. The Council feel impelled to express their strong opinion that the game of football is quite unsuitable for females and ought not to be encouraged ... The Council request the clubs belonging to the Association to refuse the use of their grounds for such matches."

It was more than just a request. The announcement meant that women would no longer be allowed to play soccer in any British stadium if it was home to a men's team that belonged to the Football Association. In other words, "No Girls Allowed."

But British women didn't just pick up their soccer balls and go home. Fifty-eight women's teams got together almost immediately to form the British Ladies Football Association (BLFA). Beginning in March 1922 and lasting until June 24, 1922, a championship tournament was held by 23 of those women's teams. Some of these teams had their own fields to play on, and some of the games were played on rugby fields.

Though efforts were made to keep it alive, the BLFA played for only one season. Still, British women continued to play soccer even though the ban by the Football Association lasted until 1971! Many other European countries had established leagues for women as far back as the 1930s, and by the time the British ban was lifted, almost 35 other countries had women's leagues or national teams.

ABBY WAMBACH

ABBY WAMBACH

NO PLAYER IN SOCCER HISTORY—male or female—has scored more goals in international matches than Abby Wambach. Wambach was a member of the U.S. national women's team from 2001 to 2015. In that time she played 256 games and scored 184 goals. Wambach grew up in Rochester, New York, where she was the youngest of seven children. In a family of athletes, being the youngest meant she really had to learn how to compete! When she was young, Wambach taught herself to beat defenders by heading the ball over them and running around them. Growing up to be 5'11" (1.8 m), Wambach made the header her signature move. Leaping above opposing players, or diving towards the net, Wambach scored many of her greatest goals by using her head.

WHEN SHE WAS YOUNG, **WAMBACH TAUGHT HERSELF TO BEAT DEFENDERS** BY HEADING THE BALL OVER THEM AND RUNNING AROUND THEM.

Women's Soccer in the United States

When it comes to women's soccer, Americans are among the best in the world. The United States has won the Women's World Cup more than any other country, and has won more Olympic gold medals than anyone else in women's soccer, too. Today, there are more girls registered to play youth soccer in the United States than in all the other countries in the world combined! What makes all this even more amazing is the late start that women's soccer got in the United States.

In 1922, the Dick Kerr Ladies soccer team came to America. They were the best women's soccer team in England, but when they got to the United States they found that there were no established women's teams to play against. So the Dick Kerr Ladies had to play against men's teams. They played seven games against teams in the American Soccer League and posted three wins, two losses, and two ties. Pretty impressive!

Still, few girls and women played soccer in the United States right up into the 1960s. Even for those who did play it, soccer was only seen as a fun way to get a little exercise. It wasn't taken very seriously at all.

The first real league for women was a church league set up in St. Louis, Missouri, in 1951. It was called the Craig Club Girls Soccer League. It had four teams and lasted for two seasons. But it wasn't until the 1970s that women's soccer began to take off. New laws were passed in 1972 that said that American universities had to spend the same amount of money on women's sports as they spent on men's sports. Suddenly, women's college soccer began to grow. As it did, more and more girls started playing youth and high school soccer, too. By 1985, there were so many women playing soccer that it made sense to have an American national team. It was slow going for the first couple of years, but soon young stars such as Mia Hamm and Brandi Chastain were added to the team. Those two, along with veteran Michelle Akers, led the United States to victory at the first Women's World Cup in 1991. People were starting to pay attention now!

A gold medal at the 1996 Olympics in Atlanta, Georgia, gave U.S. women's soccer another boost, but the big breakthrough came when the Americans won the Women's World Cup again, at home, in 1999. The final game against China on July 10, 1999, was a thriller. Over 90,000 fans packed the Rose Bowl in Pasadena, California, setting a worldwide attendance record for any women's sports event. The U.S. beat China 1–0, and Brandi Chastain's winning goal on the final penalty kick was a moment that no one who saw it will ever forget.

Women's soccer in the United States was finally moving beyond just the college ranks. Since the late 1990s, a few different professional leagues have started up. Since 2013, the National Women's Soccer League (NWSL) has been the top spot for female players in North America. The NWSL is a 10-team league featuring national team players from Canada, Mexico, and the United States.

MICHELLE AKERS

WHEN IT COMES TO WOMEN'S SOCCER, AMERICANS ARE AMONG THE BEST IN THE WORLD.

HAMM DRIVING TOWARD THE GOAL AGAINST THE BRAZILIAN NATIONAL TEAM

CHASTAIN CELEBRATING THE WINNING SHOT OF THE WOMEN'S 1999 WORLD CUP FINAL

NATIONAL WOMEN'S SOCCER LEAGUE

The clubs in the league are:

- ➡ Boston Breakers
- ➡ Chicago Red Stars
- ➡ Houston Dash
- ➡ FC Kansas City
- ➡ North Carolina Courage
- ➡ Orlando Pride
- ➡ Portland Thorns FC
- ➡ Seattle Reign FC
- ➡ Sky Blue FC (New Jersey)
- ➡ Washington Spirit

THE U.S. WOMEN'S TEAM CELEBRATES AN OLYMPIC GOLD IN 1996.

WOMEN'S SOCCER STARS

Not all of the best women's soccer players in the world come from North America, but many of the ones who represent Canada and the United States in international tournaments also play for teams in the National Women's Soccer League.

CARLI LLOYD is from Delran, New Jersey. She's been playing soccer since she was five years old and started playing on co-ed teams with boys. Lloyd's gone on to win Olympic gold medals in 2008 and 2012. In 2015, she was named the FIFA Player of the Year. She led the U.S. to the Women's World Cup that year, with three goals in a 5–2 win over China in the championship game. Lloyd is the first woman, and just the second player ever, to score a hat trick in the World Cup final. She also scored the only goal in a 1–0 win over Brazil in the 2008 Olympic gold medal game, and had both goals in a 2–1 win over Japan in the 2012 gold medal game. A star at Rutgers University, Lloyd's played for the NWSL since 2013 with the Western New York Flash and the Houston Dash.

CARLI LLOYD

ALEX MORGAN grew up in Diamond Bar, California, not far from Los Angeles. At 22 years old, she was the youngest player on the U.S. women's national team at the 2011 Women's World Cup. A year later, she scored the winning goal in a thrilling semifinal against Canada at the 2012 Olympics in London, England, en route to winning the gold medal. In all, Morgan played 31 games for the U.S. women's team in 2012 and had 28 goals and 21 assists. She joined the legendary Mia Hamm as the only American women to top 20 goals and 20 assists in one year and was named the U.S. Soccer Female Athlete of the Year. In 2015, Morgan helped the United States win the Women's World Cup. Leading up to the 2016 Olympics, she scored the fastest goal ever in a CONCACAF qualifying tournament with a goal just 12 seconds into a 5–0 win over Costa Rica. She's played in the NWSL since its first season of 2013 as a member of Portland Thorns FC and the Orlando Pride.

ALEX MORGAN

MEGAN RAPINOE

MEGAN RAPINOE was born and raised in Redding, California. She was one of six children, including her twin sister Rachael, and played youth soccer on a team coached by her father. When they were in high school, the twin sisters played with an amateur team that played against pros in the Women's Premier Soccer League. Rapinoe began playing with the U.S. women's national team in 2006. She gained instant fame among soccer fans during the quarterfinals of the 2011 Women's World Cup when, in the dying seconds of extra time, she lifted a long crossing pass that was headed in for the winning goal by Abby Wambach. A year later, Rapinoe scored two goals to lead the United States past Canada in a thrilling semifinal at the 2012 Olympics in London, England, on the way to winning the gold medal. In 2015, Rapinoe helped the United States win the Women's World Cup. She has played with Seattle Reign FC in the NWSL since its first season of 2013 and has also played with club teams in Australia and France.

Canadian **CHRISTINE SINCLAIR** is one of the greatest players in the world. Only American Abby Wambach has scored more international goals in the history of soccer—men's or women's. Sinclair has been a member of the Canadian national women's team since 2000, when she was just 16 years old. When she scored the winning goal in a 2–1 victory over Brazil in the bronze medal game at the 2016 Olympics, Sinclair was playing in her 250th international match. The longtime captain of Canada's team was the leading scorer at the 2012 Olympics, when Canada also won a bronze medal. She played at the Women's World Cup in 2003, 2007, 2011, and 2015. Two of Sinclair's uncles played professional soccer, and growing up in Burnaby, British Columbia, she started playing when she was only four years old. She became well known to American soccer fans while playing at the University of Portland from 2001 to 2005 and leading the school to two NCAA championships. Sinclair has been a member of Portland Thorns FC since the NWSL's first season. She appeared on the cover of the Canadian version of the FIFA 2016 video game along with international star Lionel Messi.

CHRISTINE SINCLAIR

GET IN THE GAME

IT'S VERY HARD to make your living as a professional athlete. It takes years of dedication to your sport ... and it takes some luck, too. Even if you make it all the way, an injury could end your career at any time. Most athletes last a very short time at the highest level of their game. Then they have to find another job. That's why parents and teachers so often say that you have to stay in school!

You've probably never heard of the highest-paid athlete in sports history. He was a chariot racer in ancient Rome named Gaius Appuleius Diocles. Diocles lived during the second century A.D. and is said to have earned almost 36 million Roman sesterces. That would be worth about $15 billion today!

We're never going to see an athlete earn that kind of money, but for the select few who are the best in the world at what they do, a sports career can be very rewarding—especially if you're a European soccer player!

LIONEL MESSI

Top 10 Athlete Earnings in 2016

PLAYER	SPORT	SALARY	ENDORSEMENTS	TOTAL
Cristiano Ronaldo	Soccer	$56 million	$32 million	$86 million
Lionel Messi	Soccer	$53.4 million	$28 million	$81.4 million
LeBron James	Basketball	$23.2 million	$44 million	$72.2 million
Roger Federer	Tennis	$7.8 million*	$60 million	$67.8 million
Kevin Durant	Basketball	$20.2 million	$36 million	$56.2 million
Novak Djokovic	Tennis	$21.8 million*	$34 million	$55.8 million
Cam Newton	Football	$41.1 million°	$12 million	$53.1 million
Phil Mickelson	Golf	$2.9 million*	$50 million	$52.9 million
Jordan Spieth	Golf	$20.8 million*	$32 million	$52.8 million
Kobe Bryant	Basketball	$25 million	$25 million	$50 million

CAM NEWTON

* = prize money   ° = salary + bonuses

SERENA WTI LIAMS

Top-earning female athlete in 2016

Tennis player
SERENA WILLIAMS

$8.9 million in prize money
$20 million in endorsements
TOTAL EARNINGS:
$28.9 MILLION

Top-paid American baseball player in 1878

BOB FERGUSON
Chicago White Stockings
Salary $3,700

Average British soccer salary in 1961

£20 PER WEEK
(Today, that would
be about £900,
or about $1,000.)

First soccer players to be paid

JOHN LOVE and
FERGUS SUTER
(Scotland) 1878–79
Salary unknown

Highest American baseball salary in 2016

CLAYTON KERSHAW
Los Angeles Dodgers
$31.2 million

CLAYTON KERSHAW

Average American baseball salary in 1961

**$19,000
PER YEAR**

Highest American baseball salary in 1961

WILLIE MAYS
San Francisco Giants
$85,000

Average American sports salaries in 2016

NBA: $5.0 million per player
MLB: $4.4 million per player
NHL: $2.4 million per player
NFL: $2.1 million per player
MLS: $316,777.33 per player
NWSL: $278,000 per team

FOR MORE SOCCER READING, CHECK OUT:

Crisfield, Deborah W. *The Everything Kids' Soccer Book.* 3rd ed. F&W Media, 2015.

Gifford, Clive. *Soccer Record Breakers.* Carlton Kids, 2017.

Hoena, Blake. *National Geographic Kids Everything Soccer.* National Geographic, 2014.

Hornby, Hugh. *DK Eyewitness Books: Soccer.* DK Children, 2010.

Zweig, Eric. *National Geographic Kids Everything Sports.* National Geographic, 2016.

QUOTATION CREDITS

page 12: Searby, Peter. *A History of the University of Cambridge,* 1750-1870. Volume 3. Cambridge University Press, 1997.

page 13: *The Field: The Country Gentleman's Newspaper.* December 14, 1861. p. 525.

page 42: Singer, P.N. *Galen: Selected Works.* Oxford University Press, 1997. pp. 299-304.

page 44: *Bulletin of the Essex Institute.* Volume XVI. Salem, MA: Essex Institute Press, 1884.

page 46: McCray, Larry. "The Amazing Francis Willughby, and the Role of Stoolball in the Evolution of Baseball and Cricket." ourgame.mlblogs.com/the-amazing-francis-willughby-and-the-role-of-stoolball-in-the-evolution-of-baseball-and-cricket-8a282d7721b6.

page 47: Cram, David, Jeffrey Forgeng, and Dorothy Johnston, eds. Francis *Willughby's Book of Games: A Seventeenth-Century Treatise on Sports, Games and Pastimes.* Routledge, 2016.

page 48: "The Same Old Game: The True Story of the Origins of the World's Football Games." football-origins.com/tag/eton.

page 50: "Did William Webb Ellis Invent Rugby?" therugbyhistorysociety.co.uk/didhe.html.

page 62: "Argentina President Says Messi 'God's gift' to Country." sports.inquirer.net/215185/messi-gods-gift-to-argentina-president.

page 69: *FIFA: 90 Minutes for Mandela.* Documentary. November 2007.

page 73: Barboza, Scott. "Credit for Patenaude Long Overdue." www.espn.com/boston/columns/story?id=5370416.

page 99: Newsham, Gail. "Dick, Kerr Ladies FC 1917-1965." www.dickkerrladies.com/page7.htm.

INDEX

Boldface indicates illustrations

A
Akers, Michelle 102, **102**
Altidore, Jozy **98,** 98–99
American League of Professional Football 96
American Soccer League (ASL) 96–97, 102
Ancient times 36, 36–39, **37, 38, 39,** 42
Arantes do Nascimento, Edson see Pelé
Argentina 24, 65, **65,** 73 74, **96–97**
Asia, boys playing soccer **8–9**
ASL (American Soccer League) 96–97, 102
Assistant referees 23
Aston, Ken 24
Attacker, defined 16

B
Baggataway (Native American game) 44
Ball 22, **22,** 24, 40–41, **40–41**
Baseball 78, **78,** 79, 107
Basketball 52, **52,** 106, 107
Batistuta, Gabriel 67, **67**
Beckenbauer, Franz 82, **98**
Beckham, David **93,** 93–96, **94, 95**
Beckham, Victoria 93
Beckham Rule (Designated Player Rule) 95, 98, 99
Belgium 72, **96**
Bend It Like Beckham (movie) 95
Bending the ball 95
Best, George 98
Bicycle kick 16, **16**
BLFA (British Ladies Football Association) 101
Bloxam, Matthew 50
Book of Plaies (Willughby) 46–47
Booked/booking 16, 24
Bosio, Edoardo 61
Box, defined 16
Bradley, Bob 99
Bradley, Michael 99, **99**
Brazil
    modern soccer 65, 68, **68**
    Olympics **57,** 104, 105
    women's team **103,** 104, 105
    World Cup **64,** 67, 70
Breakaway, defined 16
British Ladies Football Association (BLFA) 101
Bryant, Kobe 106
Bulgaria **64**
Butler, Samuel 48

C
Calcio (Italian game) **43**
Campos, Jorge 86
Canada
    Canadian Championship 91
    MLS 84, 90
    Olympics 72, **72,** 80–81
    rugby 49
    women's soccer 72, **72,** 80–81, 105
Cap 16, **16**
Caribbean region 91
Cascadia Cup 87
Caution see Yellow card
Central America 91

Charlton, Sir Bobby 59
Chastain, Brandi 102, **103**
Chelsea **21**
China, ancient **36,** 36–37
China, modern **14,** 102, 104
Clear, defined 16
Clock see Time
Coin toss **18–19**
Confederation of North, Central American, and Caribbean Association Football (CONCACAF) 91, 104
Corner kicks **12–13,** 19, 25, **25**
Costa Rica 104
Cross, defined 16
Cruyff, Johan 98
Cuju (Chinese game) 36–37, **36–37,** 41

D
D.C. United **84–85,** 85, 89, 94
Defenders, job 26
Denmark **72**
Designated Player Rule (Beckham Rule) 95, 98, 99
Dick Kerr Ladies soccer team 102
Diocles, Gaius Appuleius 106
Dive, defined 16
Djokovic, Novak 106
Donohoe, Thomas 65, 68
Donovan, Landon **90, 90,** 95
Dos Santos, Giovani 95, **95**
Draw, defined 16
Dribble/dribbling 16, **16**
Drogba, Didier 95, **95**
Durant, Kevin 106
Duration of match see Time

E
East Timor **74**
EFL (English Football League) 58–59
Egypt, ancient 38, **38**
Ellis, William Webb 50, **50**
England
    average soccer salary 107
    empire 59–60
    history of soccer 12–14, 42–48, **46,** 50, **51,** 58, 60, **100,** 100–101
    Middle Ages 42–44, 45, 60
    national team 93
    Olympics 72, **72**
    Premier League 59
    professional players 58
    rugby 49
    rules of the game 12–15, 18
    women's soccer **58, 100,** 100–101
    World Cup 24, **67**
English Football League (EFL) 58–59
Episkyros (Greek game) 38
Equipment 23
Extra time 16, **20,** 23

F
FA see Football Association
Fans (supporters) 15, **15,** 17
FC Barcelona 61, 62, **63,** 65
Fédération Internationale de Football Association (FIFA)
    Congress (Mexico, 2016) **69**

    formation 68–69
    logo **18**
    number of member countries 74
    Soccer Wars 97
    tournaments 56
    World Cup's creation 71
    zone map 76–77
Federer, Roger 106
Feint/feinting, defined 17
Ferguson, Bob 107
Ferguson, Sir Alex 59
Field of play 22, 23, **27**
FIFA see Fédération Internationale de Football Association
First Nations 44
Florie, Tom 73
Fontaine, Just 67, **67**
Football (American) 49, 79, 96–97, 106, 107
Football Association (FA) 13, 14–15, 18–19, 58, 101
Formations 26, **26**
Forwards, job 26
Fouls and misconduct **20,** 24, **24**
Fourth official 21, 23
France
    history of soccer 60
    Middle Ages 45, 60
    modern soccer 60–61
    newspaper 60
    Olympics **70,** 70–71, 72, **72**
    women's soccer **72**
Free kicks 25, **29**

G
Galen (Greek doctor) 42
Geiger, Mark
    foreword by 7
    personal soccer story 34
Germany
    history 60
    modern soccer 61–62
    Olympics 51
    Women's World Cup **57**
    World Cup 90
Goal, crossbar 15
Goal kicks 25
Goalkeepers 19, **20, 22,** 26
Golf 106
Great Depression 71, 73
Greece, ancient 38 39, 42

H
Hamm, Mia 102, **103,** 104
Harpaston (Greek game) 38–39
Harpastum (Roman game) 39, **39,** 42
Harry Potter books 52
Harvard University 49
Hat tricks 67, 73, 104
Head/heading/header 17, **17, 63,** 101
Heel, defined 17
Hinton, Harry 62
History of soccer 32–53
    1600s 46–47
    1800s 47
    ancient China **36,** 36–37
    ancient Egypt 38, **38**
    ancient Greece and Rome 38–39, 39, 42
    ball 40–41, **40–41**
    bans on soccer 46
    England 12–14, 42–48, **46,** 50, **51,** 58, 60, **100,** 100–101
    English public schools 47–48, 50
    Mesoamerica 42
    Middle Ages 42–45, 60
    mob football 44–46, **45**
    professional players 58
    recent changes 51

rules 12–15, 19
spread 60–68
women's soccer **100**, 100–105
Hockey 78, **78**, 107
Holland **70**
Huangdi (Yellow Emperor, China) 36
Hurst, Geoff **67**

I
Ibrahimović, Zlatan **58**
Injuries, adding time 21
International Football Association Board
(IFAB) 18
Italy **43, 45, 47, 48,** 61

J
James, LeBron 106
Japan 37, **37,** 104
Johannesburg, South Africa **15**
Johnston, Julie **80–81**

K
Kansas City Wizards 85
Kemari (Japanese game) 37, **37**
Kennedy, Benjamin 48
Kershaw, Clayton 107, **107**
Kit, defined 17
Kocsis, Sándor 67

L
LA Galaxy 86, **87,** 88, 90, 93, 95
La Somone, Senegal **11**
Lacrosse **44**
Lalas, Alexi 85, **87**
Laws of the Game
adding time 20–21
ball 22
ball in and out of play 24
breaking the law 23
changing 18–19
corner kicks 25
creation of 14–15
duration of match 23
field of play 22, 23, **27**
fouls and misconduct 24
free kicks 25
goal kicks 25
key changes 19
match officials 23
number of 22
offside 19, 24
outcome of match 24
penalty kicks 19, 25
players 23
players' equipment 23
referee 23
start and restart of play 23
test for referees 30–31
throw-ins 19, 25
Lloyd, Carli 10, **10**
Los Angeles Galaxy *see* LA Galaxy
Love, John 107

M
Major League Soccer (MLS)
All-Star Game 85
average salary 107
birth of 82, 84, **84–85,** 85
expansion to Canada 90
map of teams 88–89
MLS Cup 85, **87,** 90, **92–93,** 95
salary cap 95, 98
season 84–85
teams 84, 86
Manchester United **21, 58,** 59, **59,** 93
Mandela, Nelson 69, **69**
Maps
FIFA zones 76–77

MLS teams 88–89
Mark, defined 17
Mary, Queen of Scots 40
Match, defined 17
Mays, Willie 107
McBride, Brian 90
McGill University 49
Meola, Tony 85, **85**
Mesoamerica 42
Messi, Lionel 61, 62, **62,** 105, 106, **106**
Mexico **42,** 86, 90, 91
Mickelson, Phil 106
Middle Ages 42–45, 60
Midfielders, job 26
MLS *see* Major League Soccer
Mob football 44–46, **45**
Montreal Impact 89, 91
Morgan, Alex 104, **104**
Morley, Ebenezer Cobb 14, 22
Müller, Gerd 67, 98

N
Naismith, James 52
Naming the sport 13
NASL *see* North American Soccer League
National Football League (NFL) 96–97
National Women's Soccer League (NWSL)
102, 103, 107
Native Americans 44, **44**
Netherlands **70**
New England Revolution **87,** 89, 90
New York City FC **83,** 89
New York Cosmos **92,** **97,** 97–98
New York MetroStars 85
New York Red Bulls 85, 89, **92,** 98–99
Newton, Cam 106, **106**
Neymar **57**
NFL (National Football League) 96–97
Nil, defined 17
North American soccer 80–107
Beckham, David **93,** 93–96, **94, 95**
competitions 91
CONCACAF 91
Designated Players 95, 95, 98, 99
early leagues 96–98
map 88–89
MLS 82, 84–89
MLS stars 98–99, **98–99**
NASL 92
women's soccer history 100, 100–105
North American Soccer League (current)
91, 92, 97
North American Soccer League (historic)
82, 87, 97
Northern Ireland 18
NWSL *see* National Women's Soccer League

O
Offside rule 19, 24
Olympics
early years 38, **70,** 70–71, 72, **72**
today **57,** 72, **72**
women's soccer 72, **72, 80–81,** 102, **103,**
104, 105
Origins *see* History of soccer
Outcome, determining 24
Own goal, defined 17

P
Pace, defined 17
Paraguay 73
Pasuckuakohowog (Algonquian game) 44
Patenaude, Bert 73, **73,** 97
Pelé 64, **64,** 67, 82, **97,** 97–98, **98**
Penalty kicks 19, 25, **25**
Philippines **46–47**
Players
equipment 23

jobs of 26
Laws of the Game 23
top earners 106–107, **106–107**
Portugal 61, 62–63, 86
Practice 10, 44
Preston Ladies Football Club 100
Prince, Nichelle **80–81**

Q
Quidditch 52, **52**

R
Ramos, Sergio **63**
Rapinoe, Megan 105, **105**
Rapinoe, Rachael 105
Real Madrid **29,** 61, **63,** 65, 93
Red cards 19, **20,** 24, 29, **29**
Referees
adding time 20–21
Geiger's experience as **6,** 7, **7**
Laws of the Game 23
tests 30–31
training 75, **75**
World Cup 75
Rimet, Jules 71
Rome, ancient 38–39, **39,** 42
Ronaldo, Cristiano 61, **61,** 106
Rowling, J.K. 52
Rugby (sport) 13, **13,** 15, 48, **49,** 50, **50**
Rugby (town), England 48, 50
Rules
Designated Player Rule (Beckham Rule)
95, 98, 99
English public schools 48
governing organizations 15, 18–19
history 12–15, 19
see also Laws of the Game
Russia **71,** 74

S
San Jose Clash **84–85,** 85
San Jose Earthquakes 85, 88, 98
Scotland 18
Seattle Sounders 87, 88, **92–93,** 98
Sempare, Brenda **100**
Shakespeare, William 45
Shrewsbury School, England 48
Sinclair, Christine 105, **105**
Skills 10
Soccer
confederations (zones) 56, 76–77
different styles 14
maps 76–77, 88–89
origin of name 13
popularity 34, 35
spread 60–68
terms 16–17
Soccer Wars 97
South Africa 69
South Korea 86
Southampton **59**
Spain **51,** 63, 65, **74**
Spieth, Jordan 106
Sporting Kansas City 85, 89
Start and restart of play 23
Stirling, Scotland 40, **40**
Substitute players 19, 20–21
Super Bowl 79
Supporters (fans) 15, **15,** 17
Suter, Fergus 107

T
Tackle 17, **17**
Tennis 106, 107, **107**
Thimphu, Bhutan **32–33**
Throw-ins 19, **19,** 25, **25**
Time 19–21, 23
Toronto FC 89, 90, 91, **92–93,** 99

Touch, defined 17
Touchline, defined 17
Travel team, defined 17

U
Ulama (Mexican game) 42, **42**
United Kingdom
    average soccer salary 107
    empire 59–60
    rules of the game 18
    see also England
United Soccer League (USL) 92, 97, 102, 107
United States
    CONCACAF **80–81**, 91
    Olympics 72, **72**, **80–81**, **103**
    women's soccer 72, **72**, **80–81**, 102–103, **103**, 104, 105
    Women's World Cup 102, 104, 105
    World Cup 73, **73**, 82, 84, **84**, 85, 86, 90, **96–97**
    see also Major League Soccer
Uruguay 70, **70**, 71, 73–74
U.S. Open Cup 91, 92
U.S. Soccer Federation 84, 97
USL see United Soccer League (USL)

V
Valderrama, Carlos 86, **86**
Vancouver Whitecaps 87, 88, 91, 98
Veteran players 23
Vikings 43–44
Villa, David **83**, 95
Villarreal of La Liga 99

W
Wales 18
Wambach, Abby 101, **101**, 105
Williams, Serena 107, **107**
Willughby, Francis 46–47
Winner, determining 24
Women's soccer
    CONCACAF **80–81**
    England **58**
    history **100**, 100–105
    Laws of the Game 23
    Olympics 72, **72**, **80–81**, 102, **103**, 104, 105
    stars 104–105, **104–105**
Women's World Cup **57**, 102, **103**, 104, 105
World Cup
    attendance 79
    bids to host 71
    facts 67
    hat tricks 67, 73, 104
    by the numbers 66
    origins 70–71, 73–74
    qualification matches 74
    referees 75
    today 74–75
    trophy 74, **74**
World Cup (1930) 73, **96–97**, 97
World Cup (1966) 24, **64**, **67**
World Cup (1970) 24
World Cup (1994) 82, 84, **84**
World Cup (2002) 86, 90
World Cup (2010) 74
World Cup (2014) **54–55**, 70
World Cup (2018) 74
Wudu (Han Emperor, China) 37
Wynalda, Eric 85, **85**, 86

Y
Yellow card (caution) 16, 19, 20, 24, 28, **28**
Yellow Emperor, China 36
Youth players, rules 23

Z
Zone map 76–77

CREDITS

ASP: Alamy Stock Photo; BI: Bridgeman Images; GI: Getty Images; NGC: National Geographic Creative; SS: Shutterstock

Cover (UP), Daxiao Productions/SS; (RT), tratong/SS; (LO CTR), Metin Pala/Anadolu Agency/GI; (LO LE), strickke/GI; Back Cover, Masakazu Watanabe/Aflo Co., Ltd./ASP; Spine, irin-k/SS; 1, Steve Bronstein/GI; 2-3, Hero Images/GI; 4 (UP RT), Igor Terekhov/GI; 4 (CTR RT), Christophe Boisvieux/GI; 4 (LO RT), Sitade/GI; 4 (CTR LE), siribao/SS; 5 (UP LE), GI; 5 (UP CTR), Dirk Rietschel/GI; 5 (UP RT), Scott Halleran/GI; 5 (LO CTR), goir/GI; 5 (LO LE), irin-k/SS; 6, Alex Grimm/FIFA/FIFA via GI; 7 (UP LE), Igor Terekhov/GI; 7 (UP RT), irin-k/SS; 7 (LO), Victor Decolongon/GI; 8-9, siribao/SS; 10 (UP), Metin Pala/Anadolu Agency/GI; 10 (LO), BK foto/SS; 11 (UP LE), Andreas Gradin/SS; 11 (UP RT), Mile Atanasov/ASP; 11 (LO), Tino Soriano/NGC; 12 (LE), vgajic/GI; 12 (RT), Steven King/Icon Sportswire/Corbis via GI; 13 (LO LE), Ramsey Cardy/Sportsfile via GI; 13 (UP RT), Barcin/GI; 14 (UP), PA Images/ASP; 14 (LO), Stanley Chou/FIFA/FIFA via GI; 15 (UP LE), GILKIS/Alana Meyer/GI; 15 (CTR RT), Photo by Friedemann Vogel/FIFA/FIFA via GI; 16 (UP), Stu Forster/GI; 16 (CTR LE), David Edsam/ASP; 16 (LO RT), Maxisport/SS; 17 (UP), David Alan Harvey/NGC; 17 (CTR LE), goir/GI; 17 (LO RT), Dragan Ristovski/ASP; 18 (UP), aslu/Ullstein Bild via GI, 18 (LO LE), Laurence Griffiths/GI; 18 (LO RT), Sascha Steinbach/UEFA/UEFA via GI; 19, Alexa Reyes/AFP/GI; 20 (UP), dpa Picture Alliance Archive/ASP; 20 (CTR), Doug Pensinger/GI; 20 (LO), Richard Heathcote/GI; 21, Darren Walsh/Chelsea FC via GI; 22 (CTR), adventtr/GI; 22 (LO LE), dslaven/SS; 22 (LO RT), Tim McGuire/GI; 23 (UP RT), Photo by Friedemann Vogel/FIFA/FIFA via GI; 23 (CTR), Oktay Ortakcioglu/GI; 23 (LO), photoDISC; 24, Laszlo Szirtesi/SS; 25 (UP), Masakazu Watanabe/Aflo Co., Ltd./ASP; 25 (CTR), Amy Myers/SS; 25 (LO), Masakazu Watanabe/Aflo Co., Ltd./ASP; 26 (UP), darikuss/SS; 26 (CTR), darikuss/SS; 26 (LO), darikuss/SS; 27 (BACKGROUND), antpkr/SS; 28 (UP RT), Joern Pollex/FIFA/FIFA via GI; 28 (LO), Icon Sportswire via AP Images; 28 (UP LE), Kaesler Media/SS; 29 (UP LE), Alex Livesey/GI; 29 (CTR RT), Alex Grimm/FIFA/FIFA via GI; 29 (LO), Gines Romero/SS; 30 (UP LE), irin-k/SS; 30 (UP RT), DragonImages/GI; 30 (LO), Paolo Bona/SS; 31 (UP), Igor Terekhov/GI; 31 (LO), Chones/SS; 32-33, Christophe Boisvieux/GI; 34 (UP), Metin Pala/Anadolu Agency/GI; 34 (LO), DK foto/SS; 35 (UP LE), Design Pics Inc/NGC; 35 (UP RT), Mile Atanasov/ASP; 35 (LO), Alex Livesey/FIFA/FIFA via GI; 36 (LO LE), Qian Xuan/Pictures from History/BI; 36 (LO RT), Zhang Peng/LightRocket via GI; 37 (UP CTR), Xinhua/Zhu Zheng/ASP; 37 (LO), Chinese School/National Football Museum/BI; 38, DEA/G. Sioen/GI; 39 (UP), De Agostini Picture Library/GI; 39 (LO), GrashAlex/SS; 40 (UP), Danny Lawson/PA Images/ASP; 40 (LO RT), National Football Museum/BI; 40 (LO LE), National Football Museum/BI; 41 (UP LE), National Football Museum/BI; 41 (UP RT), Xinhua/Zhu Zheng/ASP; 41 (CTR RT), National Football Museum/BI; 41 (LO), National Football Museum/BI; 41 (CTR LE), National Football Museum/BI; 42, Jim Sugar/GI; 43 (UP), Fernando Bertelli/Bibliotheque des Arts Decoratifs/Archives Charmet/BI; 43 (CTR), Friedemann Vogel/FIFA/FIFA via GI; 43 (LO), matimix/SS; 44 (UP), Smithsonian American Art Museum, Washington, DC/Art Resource, NY; 44 (LO), Daniel Padavona/Dreamstime; 45, Giovanni Stradano/De Agostini Picture Library/G. Nimatallah/GI; 46 (LO LE), George Hunt, Isaac Robert Cruikshank/Bonhams/BI; 46-47 (LO CTR), Jose Honorato Lozano/Christie's Images/BI; 47 (UP), Popperfoto/GI; 47 (LO RT), Cameraphoto Arte, Venice/Art Resource, NY; 48 (UP), Giovanni Grevembroch/De Agostini Picture Library/A. Dagli Orti/BI; 48 (CTR), HIP/Art Resource, NY; 49 (UP), Bob Thomas/Popperfoto/GI; 49 (LO), Popperfoto/GI; 50 (LO LE), Chris Hellier/GI; 50 (LO LE), Pictorial Press Ltd/ASP; 51 (UP), Joern Pollex/FIFA/FIFA via GI; 51 (LO RT), SZ Photo/Scherl/BI; 51 (LO LE), Suddeutsche Zeitung/Granger, NYC—All rights reserved; 52 (UP LE), irin-k/SS; 52 (CTR RT), Yobro10/Dreamstime; 52 (LO), Adwo/SS; 53 (UP CTR), Sitade/GI; 53 (UP RT), Image Ideas; 53 (CTR LE), Michael Flippo/Dreamstime; 53 (LO RT), Image Ideas; 53 (LO), Grafissimo/GI; 54-55, 56 (UP), Metin Pala/Anadolu Agency/GI; 56 (LO), BK foto/SS; 57 (UP LE), Frederic J. Brown/AFP/GI; 57 (UP RT), Mile Atanasov/ASP; 57 (LE), Joan Catuffe/GI; 58 (LE), Gircke/Ullstein Bild via GI; 58-59 (LO), Uli Scartt/AFP/GI; 59 (UP), Ben Radford/Corbis via GI; 59 (LO RT), Bob Thomas/Popperfoto/GI; 60 (UP), Archive Dresden Football Museum; 60 (CTR), Leemage/GI; 60 (LO), Ullstein Bild/Ullstein Bild via GI; 61, Carlos Rodrigues/GI; 62, Alex Caparros/GI; 63 (UP), Angel Martinez/Real Madrid via GI; 63 (LO), Popperfoto/GI; 64 (UP), an Mckelvy/The LIFE Picture Collection/GI; 64 (LO LE), A. and I. Kruk/SS; 64 (LO RT), Popperfoto/GI; 65 (UP), Anton_Ivanov/SS; 65 (LO), Gabriel Rossi/LatinContent/GI; 66 (UP LE), Bob Wilson/SS; 66 (trophies), Chones/SS; 67 (UP LE), Offside Sports Photography/ASP; 67 (UP RT), zentilia/SS; 67 (CTR), Phil Cole/Allsport/GI; 67 (LO LE), Popperfoto/GI; 68 (LF), Friedemann Vogel/GI; 69 (CTR RT), Chris Johns/NGC; 69 (LO LE), Alfredo Estrella/AFP/GI; 69 (LO RT), Humbak/ASP; 70, Popperfoto/GI; 71 (UP LE), Friedemann Vogel/FIFA/FIFA via GI; 71 (UP RT), Laurence Griffiths/GI; 71 (LO CTR), Jasper Juinen/GI; 72 (UP LE), IOC Olympic Museum/Allsport/GI; 72 (UP RT), Bob Thomas/Popperfoto/GI; 72 (LO LE), Ronald Martinez/GI; 72 (LO RT), Miguel Medina/AFP/GI; 73, Bob Thomas/Popperfoto/GI; 74 (UP), Jamie McDonald/GI; 74 (LO), Mohd Rasfan/AFP/GI; 75 (UP), Joern Pollex/FIFA/FIFA via GI; 75 (LO), Steve Bardens/FIFA/FIFA via GI; 76-77, NG Maps; 78 (UP LE), irin-k/SS; 78 (UP RT), GraphicaArtis/GI; 78 (CTR RT), photoDISC; 78 (LO), photoDISC; 78 (CTR LE), photoDISC; 79 (UP RT), Rob Wilson/SS; 79 (CTR LE), Dan Thornberg/SS; 79 (LO), photoDISC; 79 (CTR RT), photoDISC; 79 (LO), Popperfoto/GI; 80-81, Scott Halleran/GI; 82 (UP), Metin Pala/Anadolu Agency/GI; 82 (LO), BK foto/SS; 83 (UP LE), Photo by Victor Decolongon/GI; 83 (LO), Mile Atanasov/ASP; 84 (UP), Michael Stewart/GI; 84 (LO LE), goir/GI; 84 (LO RT), AP Photo/Lois Bernstein; 84-85 (LO CTR), George Tiedemann/GI; 85 (CTR), Doug Pensinger/GI; 86 (UP), Friedemann Vogel/FIFA/FIFA via GI; 86 (LO), Boris Horvat/AFP/GI; 87 (UP), Winslow Townson/Sports Illustrated/GI; 87 (LO), ZUMA Press, Inc./ASP; 88-89 (map), NG Maps; 88-89 (all logos), Courtesy Major League Soccer; 90, Victor Decolongon/GI; 91 (UP), Claus Andersen/GI; 91 (LO), Ricky Fitchett/ZUMA Wire/Alamy Live News; 92 (UP), Ira Black/GI; 92 (LO), Rich Graessle/Icon Sportswire/Corbis via GI; 93, Adidas via GI; 94 (UP), Nick Laham/GI; 94 (LO), Friedemann Vogel/FIFA/FIFA via GI; 95 (UP CTR), Stephen Dunn/GI; 95 (CTR RT), Rich Graessle/Icon Sportswire via GI; 95 (LO), Shaun Clark/GI; 96 (CTR), richjem/GI; 96 (LO LE), PA Images/ASP; 96 (LO RT), PA Images/ASP; 97 (UP), Eric Schweikardt/Sports Illustrated/GI; 97 (LO), George Tiedemann/Sports Illustrated/GI; 98 (UP LE), traveler1116/GI; 98 (LO RT), Rafa Rivas/AFP/GI; 99 (UP LE), Victor Decolongon/GI; 99 (LO RT), Jamie Squire/GI; 100 (UP), Popperfoto/GI; 100 (LO LE), Keystone/Hulton Archive/GI; 100 (LO RT), Bob Thomas/GI; 101, Christian Petersen/GI; 102, AP Photo/Chen Guo; 103 (UP LE), Tony Ranze/AFP/GI; 103 (UP RT), Roberto Schmidt/AFP/GI; 103 (LO), Bob Thomas/GI; 104 (LO LE), Elsa/GI; 104 (LO RT), Rich Lam/GI; 106 (UP LE), irin-k/SS; 106 (UP RT), Maxisport/SS; 106 (LO LE), Dustin Bradford/GI; 107 (UP LE), Leonard Zhukovsky/SS; 107 (UP RT), Lisa Mckown/Dreamstime; 107 (CTR), Dirk Rietschel/GI; 107 (CTR RT), Photo Works/SS; 107 (LO RT), iStockphoto/GI; 107 (LO LE), Iasha/SS

For Lennon. Welcome to the world! —EZ

Thank you, Mother, for introducing me to soccer and for being my biggest supporter
through my entire career. I know you are always looking down and cheering me on. —MG

Copyright © 2018 National Geographic Partners, LLC

Published by National Geographic Partners, LLC. All rights reserved. Reproduction of the whole or any part of the contents without written permission from the publisher is prohibited.

Since 1888, the National Geographic Society has funded more than 12,000 research, exploration, and preservation projects around the world. The Society receives funds from National Geographic Partners, LLC, funded in part by your purchase. A portion of the proceeds from this book supports this vital work. To learn more, visit natgeo.com/info.

NATIONAL GEOGRAPHIC and Yellow Border Design are trademarks of the National Geographic Society, used under license.

For more information, visit nationalgeographic.com, call 1-800-647-5463, or write to the following address:

National Geographic Partners
1145 17th Street N.W.
Washington, D.C. 20036-4688 U.S.A.

Visit us online at nationalgeographic.com/books

For librarians and teachers: ngchildrensbooks.org

More for kids from National Geographic:
kids.nationalgeographic.com

For information about special discounts for bulk purchases, please contact National Geographic Books Special Sales: specialsales@natgeo.com

For rights or permissions inquiries, please contact National Geographic Books Subsidiary Rights: bookrights@natgeo.com

Hardcover ISBN: 978-1-4263-3008-7
Reinforced library binding ISBN: 978-1-4263-3009-4

Acknowledgments
Thank you to Mark Geiger, not only for his expertise but for his enthusiasm. Thank you to Shelby Alinsky and Grace Hill Smith for their editorial assistance, and to Pinar Taskin. —EZ

The author and publisher also wish to thank the book team: Shelby Alinsky, editor; Kathryn Williams, editorial assistant; Grace Hill Smith, project manager; Amanda Larsen, art director; Sarah J. Mock and Hilary Andrews, photo editors; Joan Gossett, production editor; and Anne LeongSon and Gus Tello, design production assistants.

Printed in China
17/RRDS/1